Photo taken in garden of Mr. F. Cleveland Morgan, near Montreal, Can.

NORTHERN LADY FERN

Athyrium angustum

Field Book of Common Ferns

for identifying fifty conspicuous species of Eastern America, with directions for their culture

By

Herbert Durand

Author of "My Wild Flower Garden," etc.

With 54 Illustrations from Photographs Showing the Ferns in Their Natural Homes, and 52 Cuts from Outline Drawings

G. P. Putnam's Sons
New York and London

FIELD BOOK OF COMMON FERNS

Revised Edition
1949

Fifteenth Impression

Made in the United States of America

TO ALL

WHO FOLLOW THE LONG BROWN PATH

Here are fifty fascinating ferns of the wild, whose ancestry antedates Adam by unnumbered eons, and whose myriads of fair and friendly children await your coming in every field and every forest, by every stream and on every mountain. Their ways are truly ways of pleasantness and the path to their dwelling places is a path of perfect peace. May this unpretentious Field Book of Ferns spur you to follow this path with eyes opened to the exquisite beauty that greets you on every hand.

THE MOTIF OF THIS BOOK

I HAVE tried to keep this *Field Book of Common Ferns* true to title throughout. It is meant to be carried along and consulted frequently whenever its owner goes forth to visit and study the ferns in their natural homes; so it is purposely made to fit either a masculine coat-pocket or a feminine hand-bag. Because of its compactness, the information of general interest and particularly the detailed descriptions of the fifty fern species, are given as concisely as due regard for clarity and accuracy permits.

The text contains very few purely technical expressions. In the "Glossary" of one of the most popular of the fern books, there are no less than 150 technical fern terms: in this book I have employed very few. Yet I venture to hope that the language will not be found less understandable nor less informative because the numerous technical terms have been ignored and ordinary English words used instead.

According to Mr. F. Schuyler Mathews, the late William Hamilton Gibson once said during an address that some day he hoped to write a Botany in plain English. I may unconsciously have hitched my wagon to that sort of star while compiling this book, but what I really had in

mind was merely a sort of Fern Primer that would lead to a wider knowledge and appreciation of the ferns among the uniformed. If, however, any of my critics should call it "A fern book written in plain English," I would not argue the matter with him, nor seriously consider eliminating my few technical words in future printings.

HERBERT DURAND.

BRONXVILLE, N. Y.

ABOUT NAMES

Fern nomenclature is at present in a chaotic condition, at least as regards both the common and the botanical names of many species, and is constantly changing. In the interests of uniformity, therefore, on page 191 where BOTANICAL SYNONYMS are listed the names most generally accepted are given in heavy type, and those often used are given in italics. Furthermore, since most common ferns bear widely different vernacular names in different sections of the country, those most frequently met with are mentioned in the text following the descriptions.

Closely related to the ferns are the lycopodiums, popularly called "fern allies." Those lycopodiums most often encountered are known by the vernacular names of Club Moss, Ground Pine, Running Pine, and Ground Cedar. This book includes an illustration and a brief description of four common lycopodiums.

In order to insure the accuracy of a considerable amount of data about which I was not satisfied to trust my own experience and judgment, I have consulted freely the following authorities:

Gray's *New Manual of Botany*, 7th Edition.
Bailey's *Cyclopedia of Horticulture.*
Clute's *Our Ferns in Their Haunts.*
Parsons' *How to Know the Ferns.*
Tilton's *Fern Lover's Companion*
Beecroft's *Who's Who Among the Ferns.*
American Fern Journal.

I am deeply indebted to Dr. R. C. Benedict, of the Brooklyn Botanic Garden and Editor of the *American Fern Journal,* for permission to make abstracts of several articles in that excellent and authoritative publication; also for his courtesy in going over much of my manuscript and giving me the benefit of very welcome suggestions and advice.

I also wish to acknowledge the counsel and friendly criticism of Mrs. Elizabeth G. Britton, Honorary Curator of the New York Botanical Garden. Mrs. Britton has done me the honor of showing as much interest in the preparation of this Fern book, as she did in my other two books about Wild Flowers.

Dr. Edgar T. Wherry and his fellow camera specialists of the Wild Flower Preservation Society, and the United States Department of Agriculture, at Washington, have my deepest gratitude for sending me the excellent fern photographs from which the illustrations, showing the ferns as they grow in the wild, were made. Dr. Wherry also devoted a great deal of his valuable time to compiling information for my use and to keeping me in the straight and narrow

path regarding nomenclature and other matters germane to my subject.

The excellent and accurate outline drawings from which the cuts accompanying the fern descriptions were made, are the work of Miss Mary Wilson, of Bronxville, N. Y.

CONTENTS

ILLUSTRATIONS

ILLUSTRATIONS

WHY EVERYONE SHOULD KNOW THE FERNS

To venture into a forest or to cross the open country anywhere, knowing nothing of the ferns, is like visiting an art gallery in which the finest paintings are turned to the wall. For there is nothing that grows or lives that can approach the feathery grace, the symmetry of form, or the lacy elegance of pattern of the Ferns: and to be blind to all this beauty is nothing less than calamitous.

This is a case where even a little knowledge is an excellent thing. I have been told hundreds of times by frequenters of the wild, that having learned by hook or crook to recognize and name half a dozen ferns or so, their outings, in consequence, became so rich in new zest and added interest, that they were not content until they had identified every species within reach. One enthusiastic novice said to me, "I can go over to Duden's Woods Sundays and call every fern I see by name. Why, it's like knowing everybody I meet as I walk down Fifth Avenue, and yelling at them, 'Hello, Jim!' 'Hello, Pete!' 'Hello, Annie!' A walk means much more to me now than mere physical exercise."

While a very marked and widespread interest in our native wild flowers, bushes and trees has

developed of recent years, the ferns do not yet seem to be receiving the attention they deserve. One possible reason for this is the impression of many that their study is a difficult one, and that they are not easily cultivated.

Another is the attitude of a great number of people, among them not a few wild flower lovers, to whom a fern is a fern, simply that and nothing more. A recent visitor to my wild garden who knew and named a majority of the flowering plants, even those that were not in bloom, was dumb as an oyster when I showed her my fernery. Later, upon hearing that there were sixty species and over twenty varieties of ferns growing there, she said, "I was never so surprised in all my life. I have always thought there were only three kinds of ferns—Maidenhair, Brakes and just ferns!"

As for the vast multitudes of the unseeing, those who look upon all vegetation, except possibly things like cabbages and sunflowers, as a conglomeration of worthless weeds, their case seems hopeless. However, the introduction of Nature study into the schools may arouse in their children a better appreciation of the natural treasures of the wild, that will atone in some degree for their own ignorance and indifference.

Converts to the ranks of the fern lovers are easiest made from the second of these classes. When one knows a Maidenhair and a Bracken, it is not difficult to make him acquainted with the Christmas Fern, the Cinnamon Fern and other conspicuous kinds. And so he soon gets on

speaking terms with a goodly number and is in a fair way to become an addict.

It is a little more difficult to persuade those of the first group that the study of ferns is really one of the simplest and most delightful pursuits in the world, and that they can be grown in the home garden and grounds as easily as one can grow Zinnias, but it can be done. All that is necessary is to tell them how to go about it, and induce them to make a start, if only with a few plants. This in a nutshell is the purpose of this book.

GETTING ACQUAINTED

The way to begin even a casual acquaintance with the ferns is to visit their natural homes and see them growing in the wild. Take along a copy of this book: it will prove a wonderful help in identifying them. If you are one of the multitude of good people who know nothing at all about plants, you should first learn to distinguish ferns from flowering plants with fern-like foliage. I have a list of some forty wild flowers, cultivated plants and common garden weeds that are constantly being mistaken for ferns. Here are some of the most noticeable ones:

WILD PLANTS

Hillside Rue (Taken for Maidenhair)
Wild Columbine (Taken for Maidenhair)
Rue Anemone (Taken for small Maidenhair)

Dutchman's Breeches	Squirrel Corn
Several Native Buttercups	Poison Hemlock
Sweet Cicely	Wood Betony
Yarrow	Cow Vetch
Goosegrass and other Bed-straws	
Herb Robert	Meadow Rue (young plants

Sweet fern (A Bush of the Bayberry family)
Ground Pine and Running Pine (Fern Allies)

COMMON WEEDS

Wild Carrot	Cut-leaved Ragweed
Butter and Eggs	Tansy
Cypress Spurge	Jerusalem Oak

The so-called Asparagus Fern of the florists and the curled Parsley of kitchen gardens also belong in this category; and there are many other less conspicuous plants that occasionally cause confusion.

If the novice will remember the following three distinctive characteristics of Ferns, he will have no difficulty in telling them from all other plants at sight.

(1) Ferns never bear flowers.

(2) Instead of seeds, ferns preduce fruit-dots, or spore-cases that contain spores from which new ferns develop. (See page 28.)

(3) Usually the young leaves or fronds of ferns are at first coiled tightly like watch-springs and uncoil as the fronds continue to grow larger. However, the Grape ferns and the Rattlesnake ferns are folded in the bud and not coiled.

Early spring, before they have sent up the stems which carry the blossoms, is the time when flowering plants with deeply cut foliage are most likely to be mistaken for ferns. A glance at the new growth of leaves, however, will quickly settle the matter. Unless the tips are coiled in a circle, they are flowers. As the season advances the appearance of buds and blossoms removes all doubt and even after the blossoms have faded and gone, the fruit-dots and spore-cases tell by their presence or absence which plants are ferns and which are not.

Having learned to tell ferns at sight from other plants, the next step is to identify and name different species. The simplest way to do this is

to study the shape of the fruit-dots and the way they are arranged on the underside of the fronds. Then compare this information with the data concerning each fern, on pages 89 to 189 until the right one is found.

The following abstract of an article in the *American Fern Journal* is worth reading and thoroughly digesting in this connection:

The fruit-dots or the sori are the most characteristic and most important factors in determining identity. They are to be found, on most ferns, on the underside of ordinary fern leaves or fronds. Fronds that have them are called fertile; those without are called sterile. They vary widely in shape, size and position.

On the Common Polypody, they are round, conspicuous, yellow or brownish when mature and so large that they almost cover the pinnules on which they grow. On other ferns, the Hay-scented Fern, and the American Shield Fern, or Fancy Fern, of the florist, for example, they are so small as to be hardly noticeable without close scrutiny. On the Marginal Shield Fern they are located along and very near the margin. All of the Spleenworts, and the Lady Ferns as well, have elongated or oblong fruit-dots, as do both Chain Ferns, and on the latter they grow in rows end to end, resembling links in a chain. The fertile fronds of several species are so contracted that they are quite unlike the sterile fronds in appearance. This is notably the case with the Bracken, the Marsh Fern, and the Christmas Fern. Indeed the upper half of the fertile fronds of the latter are so narrowed that

they have given it the common name "Dagger Fern" in some sections.

The fertile fronds of the so-called "flowering" ferns, which of course have no real flowers, are usually very puzzling to beginners. The Cinnamon Fern, in June, sends up a number of spikes, covered at their tips with cinnamon-colored fruit-dots, which resemble at a distance, flower stalks something like those of the mullein. The Royal Fern has similar spikes, but they appear only at the tips of otherwise normal fronds. On the Interrupted Fern, from two to four pairs of pinnæ at the middle of the fertile frond, become very much contracted and, when the fruit-dots they bear are mature, turn black and soon wither. This leads many observers to think they have been attacked by some kind of blight. The fertile fronds of the Sensitive Fern, the Ostrich Fern, the Grape Ferns and the Rattlesnake Fern, which are also peculiar in shape and color, as well as in the arrangement of the fruit-dots, are described in detail on the pages devoted to those species.

If, after noting the size, shape and location of the fruit-dots which one sees on a wild specimen and finding a species in the book with which they seem to agree, there is still doubt as to whether the identification is correct, further comparisons can be made with the descriptions as to; (a) the length and cutting or division of the frond, (b) the character of the rootstock, (c) the nature of the surroundings in which it grows and (d) any special distinguishing mark mentioned.

With ferns, familiarity breeds enthusiasm, never contempt. One of the earliest manifestations of this feeling is a desire to collect enough specimens to fill a herbarium. To encourage this most fascinating diversion, a special article telling how to collect, press and mount specimens and how to arrange and preserve them will be found elsewhere.

FERN FACTS AND FANCIES

There are about six thousand known species of ferns scattered throughout the world, most of them in tropical countries. Geologists tell us that this is a mere handful compared with the innumerable species that flourished when the earth was young. It is not to be doubted that in the course of ages ferns were evolved from marine plants and that flowering plants were, in turn, evolved from ferns. So they are inconceivably older than any form of terrestrial vegetation now in existence. Their fossil remains have been found occasionally in the Devonian rocks, but are most abundant in those of the Carboniferous period. The coal that is mined today is composed almost entirely of ferns and their allies, which it is estimated lived and flourished and in fact constituted the only vegetation on the earth fifty-three million years or so ago. The first flowering plants did not put in an appearance until nearly thirty million years later.

In the moist, heated atmosphere of those inconceivably remote eras the ferns attained enormous size, reaching heights of fifty feet or more in the shady half-light of the vast marshes which covered the youthful sea-born continents. Their descendants today retain the distinctive characteristics of their ancestors, equaling even

the largest of them in size in the heat and wet soil of tropical jungles. There tree ferns, that are blood brothers of the common ferns of our northern woods, still grow from thirty to fifty feet tall with trunks several inches in diameter. The thick rootstocks of our wood-ferns and others of vigorous growth, are really modified tree trunks—dwindled remnants of ancient uprightness and strength.

It is extremely interesting to learn that many fossil ferns have been found to be practically identical with familiar living species. Collectors, or rather miners, of fossils have unearthed specimens that strikingly resemble our Maidenhair, Ostrich Fern, Lady Ferns, Chain Ferns, the Hay-scented Fern, some of the Shield Ferns, the Cinnamon Fern and many others.

There is probably no country or region on earth where ferns of one or more kinds do not grow. They range in size from the lofty tropical Tree ferns, down to the wee Filmy ferns of the Gulf states and the West Indies that have fronds only an inch or two long. Many of our northern ferns are perennial in the sense that the fronds live through at least one winter and some of them are evergreen.

Ferns do not bear flowers and never have, although according to an old legend they always bloomed up to the time of the Nativity. During that marvelous happening, however, when all the other plants that were mixed with the straw in the stable put forth lovely blossoms, the ferns alone failed to do so and were, in consequence, condemned to go flowerless forever after.

During the middle ages even the most learned scientists knew little or nothing about ferns and their method of reproduction, so it is not surprising that all kinds of magical powers were attributed to them by the ignorant and superstitious multitude. When young ferns were seen to appear constantly, everywhere, although older ones bore no flowers and yielded no seed, it was perfectly natural for people to ask "Where do they come from?" and as everybody knew that other kinds of plants always produced seeds and grew from seeds, it was also natural to suppose that fern seeds must exist; but, as it could not be found, it must be invisible. Therefore if invisible seed could after all be located and gathered, it should certainly give the lucky finder the power of making *himself* invisible.

One outcome of this sort of reasoning was the fanciful story of the Blue Flower which it was said blossomed only on the eve of St. John's Day, June 24th, and made shining, golden seed which ripened at midnight. It is recorded that great numbers of believers in this tale gathered together every St. John's Eve where ferns grew plentifully, spread white cloths under the plants, uttered prayers and incantations and used every means that could be thought of to collect the seed; but there is no record of anyone having ever been successful. Scores of similar tales and legends were current in those days.

As early as the year 300 B.C. ferns were thought to have medicinal value and Diosconides an M.D. who practised in Nero's day, used the Bracken and the Male Fern in concocting pre-

scriptions. In more recent times a number of other ferns, whose names are familiar to us now, were added to the list of supposedly healing plants. The Spleenworts were so named because of their alleged efficacy in treating diseases of the spleen and the Maidenhair Spleenwort had the additional reputation of stopping hair from falling and even of making new hair grow on old bald heads. An infusion of the roots and fronds of the Common Polypody was a favorite remedy for the "blues" and for preventing "fearsome and troublesome" dreams and nightmares, and then Royal Fern was used to heal wounds and mend broken bones. Other ferns were employed to cure such minor ills as asthma, colic, colds, jaundice and mild fevers.

Today apparently the only fern that has recognized medicinal value is the Male Fern, which continues to be given as a vermifuge, as it always has been since its virtues became known to Dr. Diosconides over 2200 years ago.

The old-time botanists tried for centuries to discover the mysterious process by which ferns reproduce themselves without the aid of flowers, but it was not until the year 1848 that the puzzle was solved. Even today very few people have any idea of the life history of a fern or know anything about fern *spores*. I was in a florist's store one day when a very indignant woman walked in and demanded that a fern she had purchased the day before should be sent for and taken back immediately. When asked what the trouble was, she said the leaves were all covered with nasty brown bugs and

the florist was unable to convince her that her idea of bugs was the fern's idea of seeds.

As a matter of fact spores are microscopic and do not resemble seeds in any respect, nor do they behave like seeds. The story of the life of a new fern usually begins along in July, when numbers of small brown fruit-dots (or sori) appear on the under side of fern fronds or sometimes along their margins, or sometimes on particular leaflets (fertile pinnæ), as in the Interrupted Fern (page 79), or sometimes on separate or fertile fronds (sporophylls), as in the Sensitive Fern (page 76), the Cinnamon Fern (page 80), and the Grape Ferns (pages 81, 82, and 83). The sori vary in shape, being round, kidney-shaped, oblong, linear, curved, or star-shaped. However each shape is constant for each species of fern, and thus serves as an aid in their identification. The sori are made up of dense clusters of minute spore cases, or sporangia, each containing from forty-eight to sixty-four microscopic spores. When the spores are mature the spore cases burst open and discharge them. From a single fern plant millions of spores may be thus dispersed annually, and may travel on the wind or by other carriers for many miles. Few, however, reach a suitable spot for their development. Spores of some species must develop as soon as they are disseminated, but others may remain dormant for as long as twenty years, and then develop. Here ends the phase in the life-cycle of a fern called the Asexual or Sporophyte Generation, that is the spore-producing generation. The next phase is the Gametophyte or Sexual Genera-

tion, that is the egg and sperm producing generation. Thus ferns, in their complete life-cycle pass through what biologists term an Alternation of Generations cycle. This is shown graphically in the diagram of page 32.

The Gametophyte or Sexual Generation begins when each spore develops (not into a fern plant) but into a tiny green, flattish, usually heart-shaped structure, not at all fern-like. This is called a Prothallium. From the under surface appear many fine root-like hairs (Rhizoids), and two kinds of reproductive organs: male organs (Antheridia) each one producing many microscopic spirally-coiled single cells (sperms); and the female organs (Archegonia), each one producing a single cell (egg). Eggs and sperms may be produced on the same Prothallium, or on separate Prothallia. When fully developed, the sperms swim to, and fertilize the eggs, swimming in the film of moisture on the prothallia or the ground, by means of their lashing tails (flagella). Even a microscopic moisture-film affords them water enough for this nuptial journey. From the fertilized egg a tiny simple plant develops whose first fronds are quite unlike fern fronds. This is the young fern plant. In due time other fronds appear, which grow into the fronds of the mature fern. From three to seven years are usually required for a fern to reach reproductive maturity. Then the spore-producing sori begin to appear—and the life cycle of the fern has been completed. (See page 32.) Ferns live for many years, producing a new crop of fronds each year. Prothallia live for only three to seven

weeks. During that time they produce their eggs and sperms, and see their fertilized eggs well on the way to developing a little fern plant; after which they die and disintegrate.

Definitions of Fern Terms

It is very important that the uninformed should become familiar with and learn the meaning of the following botanical terms used to describe ferns before attempting to identify them in the wild. The outline sketches on the next page will help to make the definitions clear.

Frond:—The leaf of a fern. A *frond* may be simple (entire) like those of the Walking Fern, or compound (divided into leaflets) like those of the Christmas Fern and the Royal Fern. A *frond* that bears *fruit-dots* or *spore-cases* (see below) is called "fertile" to distinguish it from one that does not. A *frond* which does not bear *fruit-dots* is called "sterile."

Pinnate:—A *frond* that is once divided into leaflets is called *pinnate*, a Latin word which means "like a feather." If the leaflets are again divided, the *frond* is said to be *bi-pinnate.*

Pinna:—One of the primary leaflets of a compound *frond.* The plural of *pinna* is *pinnæ.*

Pinnule:—One of the leaflets of a divided *pinna.*

Midvein:—The central and most prominent vein of a *pinna* or *pinnule.*

Spore:—The minute fruit of a fern, corresponding in function to a seed, but nevertheless not a seed. (See page 28 for description of the wonderful process by which a fern develops from a *spore.*)

Spore-case:—A tiny capsule containing *spores* which splits and discharges them when ripe. Spore cases are sometimes borne on separate fronds, as for example in the Sensitive, Cinnamon, and Grape Ferns; or on particular pinnæ, as in the Interrupted and Royal Ferns.

Fruit-dots:—Small groups of *spore-cases,* of various shapes, which usually appear on the underside or along the margins of the fertile *fronds.* Their shape, position and manner of arrangement constitute a reliable guide to the identity of different species.

Habitat:—The kind of natural surroundings in which ferns and other wild plants are most likely to be found.

FERN TERMS ILLUSTRATED

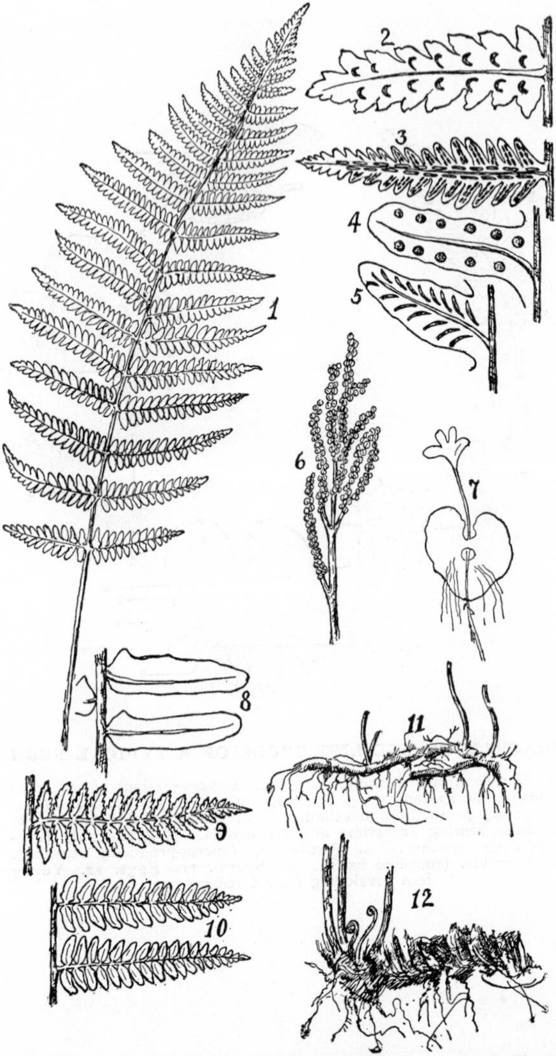

1—Frond; 2–5—Fruit-dots; 6—Fertile Frond; 7—Prothallium; 8—Pinnæ; 9, 10—Pinnules.

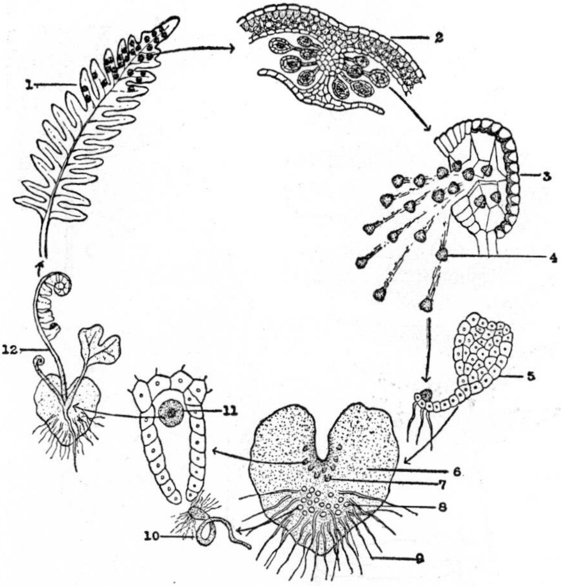

DIAGRAM OF THE LIFE-CYCLE OF A TYPICAL FERN

1. Mature frond bearing sori. 2. Cross section of a sorus showing the sporangia. 3. Sporangium shedding spores. 4. Spore. 5. Young prothallium developing from a spore. 6. Mature prothallium bearing antheridia and archegonia. 7. Archegonia (egg-producing organs). 8. Antheridia (sperm-producing organs). 9. Rhizoids. (root-like hairs). 10. Sperm. 11. Eggs. 12. Young fern developing from fertilized egg.

THE COMMON FERNS

IN THEIR NATURAL HAUNTS

Illustrations from "habitat" photographs showing the fifty pecies of Ferns and four of Club Mosses, or Lycopodiums, overed by this book, as they grow in the wild.

Photo by Dr. Paul Bartsch

COMMON POLYPODY

Polypodium virginianum

While it is found occasionally on trees and prostrate rotting logs the Common Polypody shows a decided preference for rocks. It delights to fill crevices and pockets, but is most attractive when it spreads like a carpet over the summits of huge cliffs and boulders. The fronds are of a leathery texture and stay green through at least one winter. New fronds appear in succession during spring and summer. (p. 90)

Photo by Dr. Paul Bartsch

RESURRECTION FERN

Polypodium polypodioides

The Resurrection Fern is a smaller edition of the Common Polypody and makes its home in the southern states. Indeed, the further south the fern hunter goes, the more frequently he encounters it and the higher it climbs its favorite trees. It is only up near Mason and Dixon's line that it is content to sprawl over lowly tree roots and neighboring rocks. It is called the Gray Polypody in several popular fern books. (p. 92)

Photo by Dr. Paul Bartsch

MAIDENHAIR FERN

Adiantum pedatum

It is a poor woodland that has no colonies of Maidenhair in the rich, moist soil of its more secluded and shaded recesses, especially if the dominant trees are maples, birches and beeches. The soil under cone bearing evergreens and oaks is too acid to suit its fastidious taste.

The European Maidenhair was popularly called "Virgin's Hair" in old England and it is still known in Iceland as "Freyja's Hair." (p. 94)

Photo by Dr. E. T. Wherry

VENUS'-HAIR FERN

Adiantum capillus-veneris

The Venus'-hair Fern prefers to live in the Sunny South, and reaches its best development in the Gulf States and the West Indies. The illustration shows how it drapes itself over cliffs, along the sides of deep ravines, where the rocks drip with oozing moisture and the atmosphere is saturated. A number of varieties of this fern are sold by Florists. (p. 96)

Photo by Dr. Paul Bartsch

BRACKEN

Pteridium aquilium var. *latiusculum*

Wherever the soil is sterile, sandy and dry, the Bracken is likely to flourish, whether the locality be shady or sunny. In such situations it abounds as plentifully in the old world as it does here in America.

In England, from time immemorial there has been a belief that burning the Bracken will bring rain and incidentally drive away witches. (p. 98)

Photo by Dr. C. R. Shoemaker

HAIRY LIP FERN

Cheilanthes lanosa

Where the conditions are to its liking, this fern likes to dispute with the Common Polypody the occupancy of rock clefts and pockets. It cannot be considered a rare species, as it grows abundantly where it has become established. In my garden, are a number of flourishing specimens that keep green all winter, but that may be due to the protection given them. (p. 100)

Photo by Dr. E. T. Wherry

WOOLLY LIP FERN

Cheilanthes tomentosa

This species is rare or absent north of the latitude of Washington but increases in numbers southward and becomes abundant in the Gulf States, where it is usually found on ledges and cliffs in full sun. Gray describes two other Lip Ferns—one (*C. alabamensis*) Alabama Fern with smooth fronds, frequent in the south, and the other (*C. feei*) with fronds only two or three inches long that belongs in the middle west (p. 102)

Photo taken in author's garden

PURPLE CLIFF BRAKE

Pellæa atropurpurea

The illustration shows this charming species flourishing in acid soil although Gray describes it as a dweller on dry limestone rocks.

Many fern students object to the descriptive adjective "purple" in its common name, saying that the color suggestion is really blue. And the name "brake" is meaningless. But as Gray calls it "Cliff Brake," there is nothing for me to do but acquiesce. (p. 104)

Photo by Dr. E. T. Wherry

SLENDER CLIFF BRAKE

Cryptogramma stelleri

This species has been shifted from pillar to post by the botanists, who, after taking it away from the Brackens, housed it temporarily with the Cliff Brakes and then, some thirty years or so ago, moved it over among the Rock Brakes. By the way, the difference between Cliff Brake and Rock Brake sounds like that between Tweedledum and Tweedledee, but I have no doubt that it is momentous in reality. (p. 106)

Photo by Dr. Paul Bartsch

VIRGINIA CHAIN FERN

Woodwardia virginica

The illustration indicates the difficulty of telling this from the Cinnamon Fern in the lush tangle of its swampy home. Of course, during May and early June, when the fruiting spikes of the Cinnamon Fern display their colors, there is no trouble, but after the fruiting fronds wither and disappear about July 1st, the two are like Ike and Mike—they look alike, whether a rod away or a mile. (p. 108)

Photo by Dr. C. R. Shoemaker

NARROW-LEAVED CHAIN FERN

Woodwardia areolata

This, to my mind, is a notably handsome fern and not difficult to grow in the garden in favorable locations. It will not last long, however, unless planted in very acid soil, where it is both moist and shady. A mulch of half-rotted oak leaves, or of hemlock or pine needles will be highly appreciated. (p. 110)

Photo by Dr. C. R. Shoemaker

MAIDENHAIR SPLEENWORT

Asplenium trichomanes

In sheltered localities, or if covered lightly with fallen leaves, the fronds of the Maidenhair Spleenwort remain green during the first winter, but the pinnæ wither and fall in late spring, leaving the bare stems standing amidst the new growth. The plants reach full maturity in July, when it is not unusual to find specimens with twenty to fifty of the decorative, arching fronds, though ten to fifteen is an average number. (p. 112)

Photo by Dr. C. R. Shoemaker

EBONY SPLEENWORT

Asplenium platyneuron

The Ebony Spleenwort always makes its home in the vicinity of rocks, but does not seek that intimate contact with them that the Maidenhair Spleenwort demands. It has a larger and more extensive root system and evidently requires more soil room. In the absence of fertile fronds the tuft of sterile fronds is very like that of the other. They stay green through the winter but the fertile fronds do not. (p. 114)

Photo by Dr. E. L. Crandall

NARROW-LEAVED SPLEENWORT

Athyrium pycnocarpon

The narrow-leaved Spleenwort is most attractive in eaıly summer, when the pale green fronds retain the freshness of youth, and reaches its greatest height in late August, by which time the color has changed to a much deeper green. It is our only tall common fern that is but once pinnate.

Clute reports that in some places it is called "Swamp Spleenwort" and in others "Kidney-fern," neither of which names appears to mean much. (p. 116)

Photo by Dr. Paul Bartsch

SILVERY SPLEENWORT

Athyrium thelypteroides

The Silvery Spleenwort grows in rich woods along the borders of woodland brooks and in shaded swamps. Its floral companions are usually Solomon's Plume, Trout Lilies and the Common Blue Violet. It does not occur frequently enough to be classed as common: "abundant locally" is probably a better way to put it. This fern does well in the garden in any moist shaded location if the creeping roots are not covered too deeply. (p. 118)

›to by H. G. Healy (see Frontispiece also)

NORTHERN LADY FERN

Athyrium angustum

There are so many varieties or forms of the two Lady Ferns .t it is difficult to give a comprehensive description of either. . Wherry says that in his experience the fronds of the upland cies are widest about the 5th pair of pinnæ from the bottom ile those of the lowland species are widest about the second r. And generally speaking a Lady Fern found north of ladelphia is usually the Northern. (p. 120)

Photo by Dr. Paul Bartsch

SOUTHERN LADY FERN

Athyrium asplenioides

Clute says of the Lady Fern, "while it may not be the mo abundant fern in any one locality, its wide range of habita from deep woodlands to open swamps, stony pastures a dusty roadsides, makes it common enough to be easily foun and it is certainly attractive enough to make it worth t finding."

In late summer all Lady Ferns lose their freshness a assume a dilapidated aspect. If asters are planted with the this unsightliness will be obscured. (p. 122)

Photo by Dr. C. R. Shoemaker

WALKING FERN

Camptosorus rhizophyllus

Where, as in the illustration, the Walking Fern grows in dense mats on the sloping shelves of cliffs, the plants may be cut into sods and handled in the garden, like the Polypody.

At the base of Stissing Mountain, in Duchess County, New York, there are broad ledges carpeted with the hairy-cup moss, among which the blue-green Walking Fern and the emerald Maidenhair Spleenwort vie with each other in tracing fantastic patterns. (p. 124)

Photo by Dr. C. R. Shoemaker

CHRISTMAS FERN

Polystichum acrostichoides

Although this handsome evergreen fern is still abundant in the eastern woods, it is being rapidly exterminated, because of its use for Christmas and other winter decorations.

Mr. John Robinson, of Salem, Mass., who is credited with having given the Christmas Fern its popular name, wrote, "Its mission is to cheer the winter and enhance the beauty of the other ferns by contrast." (p. 126)

Photo by Dr. E. T. Wherry

MOUNTAIN HOLLY FERN

Polystichum lonchitis

Strictly speaking the Mountain Holly Fern does not grow naturally within the territory covered by this book, but so many thousands of tourists from the "States" are now summering in the British dominions and the mountains of our own Northwest that many of my readers are certain to come across it in those distant wilds and wonder as to its identity.

It is an excellent subject for rock garden culture and can be obtained from dealers in native plants. (p. 128)

Photo by Dr. E. T. Wherry

BRAUN'S HOLLY FERN

Polystichum braunii

This handsome evergreen fern is blessed with many names. Some dealers list it as *Aspidium aculeatum braunii,* some botanists insist that its correct name is *Dryopteris braunii* and a common name frequently used is Prickly Shield Fern.

It flourishes in the shaded fernery that graces my garden, and seems entirely happy in the moist, acid, moss-covered bit of earth provided for it. It also makes a handsome showing as an individual specimen elsewhere. (p. 130)

Photo by Dr. C. R. Shoemaker.

MARSH FERN

Dryopteris thelypteris

This fern is frequently and erroneously called Lady Fern, to which it bears no resemblance at all, and in localities where the beaver exists or formerly existed it is known as the Beaver-meadow Fern. It is not difficult to cultivate but is out of place in the garden except in marshy ground or near water, and in full sun. There it looks most natural in the company of Blue-flags, Closed Gentians and Cardinal Flowers. (p. 132)

Photo by Dr. E. T. Wherry.

MASSACHUSETTS FERN

Dryopteris simulata

This fern, first recognized as a distinct species about thirt years ago, has never been given a common name by an accepte authority. Many fern books have called it Massachuset Fern, but that name was given in error, as it was actually di covered near Seabrook, New Hampshire. So, as Dr. Wherr suggests, if it must have a state name it should be New Hamp shire Fern. (p. 134)

Photo by Dr. Paul Bartsch

NEW YORK FERN

Dryopteris noveboracensis

In view of its wide distribution the name New York as applied to this fern, is another palpable misnomer, and should be replaced by a more fitting one. "Taper Fern" has been suggested as a most descriptive and appropriate substitute and has the additional merit of having been in long use among country people in many parts of the country. (p. 136)

Photo by Dr. E. L. Crandall

LONG BEECH FERN

Phegopteris polypodioides

Gray gives the habitat of this fern as damp woods, but I find it as a rule on moist rocks and cliffs, and often in full sun. And Clute says, "To find the Beech Fern in its greatest luxuriance the collector must visit the cliffs and ravines where dripping ledges provide dwelling places to its liking." (p. 138)

Photo by Dr. Paul Bartsch

BROAD BEECH FERN

Phegopteris hexagonoptera

Gray's Botany, 7th Edition, assigns no common name to this fern, but it was generally known as the Broad Beech Fern, and was so styled in all the popular books, until the compilers of Standardized Plant Names evolved the equally appropriate and perhaps more distinctive name, Winged Beech Fern. It has also been called locally the Six-angled Polypody, and Dr. Wherry tells me that "Triangle Fern" is the only name by which it is known among the mountaineers of Virginia and the Carolinas. (p. 140)

Photo by Dr. E. T. Wherry

OAK FERN

Phegopteris dryopteris

The Oak Fern is one of the most delicately beautiful members of the entire fern family. As the fronds are triangle-shaped and divided into three triangular divisions, it strikingly resembles a maniature Bracken. It rarely exceeds six to eight inches in height and is easily grown in acid soil.

Its only common name, other than Oak Fern, is, as far as known, the Three-cornered Fern, which is used in some parts of the South. (p. 142)

Photo by Dr. Paul Bartsch

MARGINAL SHIELD FERN

Dryopteris marginalis

The Marginal Shield Fern is abundant everywhere on rocky wooded hillsides and in the larger recesses of cliffs. It is particularly happy nestled between buttressed roots of big forest trees. I admire it for the symmetry of its dark blue-green fronds, which are leathery in texture, evergreen and often reach a length of 30 inches. They grow from a large, chaffy crown which protrudes an inch or two above the surface. (p. 144)

Photo by Dr. E. T. Wherry

MALE FERN

Dryopteris filix-mas

At a casual glance the Male Fern looks very like the Marginal Shield Fern, but closer inspection will disclose many differences. The most conspicuous of these are the lighter color of the fronds, the much smaller fruit-dots and their withering with the coming of frost.

The Male Fern grows wild in the Colorado Rockies, in the far Northwest and in Canada and is fairly frequent in the northern section of Maine and Vermont. (p. 146)

Photo by Dr. Paul Bartsch

GOLDIE'S FERN

Dryopteris goldiana

Aside from its stately beauty and magnificent proportions, the Goldie's Fern when grouped with other ferns of lower stature and with many colorful wild flowers, gives an almost tropical aspect to shaded situations in the wild garden. The Royal Fern, the Meadow Rue, the Turkscap Lily, the Showy Lady-slipper, the Cardinal Flower and several Woodland Asters are suggested companions, as all will flourish in the deep, moist mold it prefers. (p. 148)

Photo by Dr. E. T. Wherry

BOOTT'S SHIELD FERN

Dryopteris boottii

This species is so easily confused with other ferns that it often takes careful study to identify it. It resembles the Spinulose Shield Fern in the cutting of its fronds and the Clinton Shield Fern in general outline. Like the latter, its fertile fronds wither in autumn, while the sterile remain green all winter. If an amateur is in doubt about its identity he should compare his specimen with the outline cut and description on page 150.

Photo by Dr. Paul Bartsch

CRESTED SHIELD FERN

Dryopteris cristata

The Crested Shield Fern loves to dwell in shaded swamps among the False Hellebore and the Skunk Cabbages, where Marsh Marigolds abound and Spring Beauties, mingled with Trout Lilies, adorn the hummocks.

There are several greatly prized clumps of this neatly habited fern in my wild garden, set purposely in localities having quite different conditions of moisture, soil and exposure. It has proved remarkably adaptable and apparently is perfectly satisfied to be "just planted." (p.152)

Photo by Dr. E. T. Wherry

CLINTON'S SHIELD FERN

Dryopteris clintoniana

A well-developed specimen of the Clinton's Shield Fern is a real find and a genuine treasure for the fern garden. In the rich, deep and moist soil of its favorite haunts, it often rivals the Lady Fern in size and excels it in beauty and permanence, as its sterile fronds are practically evergreen and never lose their freshness.

Several dealers continue to list this species by its old botanical name, *Aspidium cristatum* var. *clintonianum*. (p. 154)

Photo by Dr. Paul Bartsch

SPINULOSE SHIELD FERN

Dryopteris spinulosa

Whether growing wild among rocks and boulders under evergreen trees, or in congenial corners of the home garden, or as summer decorations for porches and window boxes, this species and the two close relatives that follow are always sure to attract admiring attention. They owe their distinctive beauty to the lacy cutting of the fronds, which is as fine and intricate as that of the Hay-scented Fern; and the texture is much more substantial. (p. 156)

Photo taken in author's garden

AMERICAN SHIELD FERN

Dryopteris spinulosa var. *intermedia*

Personally, I am not enthusiastic over the common name for this beautiful species. It seems somehow that something like "Evergreen Lace Fern" would be more descriptive and more fitting. Although "common" in this case means abundant, its other definition "inferior" is apt to be inferred by those who are unfamiliar with the superior loveliness of the plant.

In catalogues this fern is likely to be listed as *Aspidium spinulosum* var. *intermedium*. (p. 158)

Photo by Dr. E. T. Wherry

MOUNTAIN SHIELD FERN

Dryopteris spinulosa var. *americana*

Broadest, brightest and best of its tribe, is this lover of the North Woods and the high mountains of Northeastern North America. Dr. Wherry states that "all of the species *Dryopteris* seem to be capable of hybridization.

Clute says this fern provides the earliest spring food of the Indians of Alaska. They dig the young, uncoiling fronds, bake them in pits heated with hot stones, and seem to keenly relish the sweetish but smoky flavor. (p. 160)

Photo by Dr. Paul Bartsch

BULBLET BLADDER FERN

Cystopteris bulbifera

The word "bladder" should be discarded as part of the common name of this fern. It doesn't belong to a plant of such refined grace. And the prefix "berry" might better have been "bulblet" and the simple name "Bulblet Fern" adopted.

The atrocious old name in general use, "Bulbiferous Bladder Fern," sounds like some hideous malformation that should be given surgical attention. (p. 162)

Photo by Dr. E. L. Crandall

COMMON BLADDER FERN

Cystopteris fragilis

This fragile little fern, which is as much at home in the tropics as in the far north, is sometimes called the Brittle Fern. First of the ferns to show its colors in early spring it soon covers the rocks and banks it frequents with fresh greenery, when all the surroundings are still sere and brown.

It is a gem for the wild garden where, if kept moist, it never shrivels until cut down by frost. (p. 164)

Photo by Dr. E. T. Wherry

RUSTY WOODSIA

Woodsia ilvensis

The Rusty Woodsia likes to establish itself on the very brink of steep cliffs where, with the early Saxifrage and various lichens, it basks in the sunshine or braves the storm and makes the best of the meager soil of its precarious location. It usually is found only after many hard climbs and fruitless searches.

Throughout the north the fronds die during winter, but in the southern states it is said to be evergreen. (p. 166)

Photo by Dr. E. T. Wherry

SMOOTH WOODSIA

Woodsia glabella

This delicate and elusive fern, while frequent in Canada, is found only rarely in this country, and always at high elevations, where temperatures are low. It can be obtained from one or two dealers in native plants and is a rarity worth having in any fernery. It has been confused with the closely related and equally rare Alpine Woodsia, but the latter has a black or brownish stem and is larger and of coarser aspect. (p. 168)

Photo by Dr. Paul Bartsch

BLUNT-LOBED WOODSIA

Woodsia obtusa

This frequenter of shady ledges and loose talus is often known as the Common Woodsia. It may be the commonest Woodsia, but it is not nearly so frequent or abundant as the Brittle Fern, with which it is so often confused. The two species are often found in company on shaded cliffs and ledges. (p. 170)

Photo by Dr. E. L. Crandall

HAY-SCENTED FERN

Dennstaedtia punctilobula

The liking of this decorative fern for rocky upland pastures is manifest to all who visit them in midsummer and see it clustered about every half-buried boulder.

Clute says it is an excellent species for cultivation in the fernery and hastens to add that it is almost impossible to eradicate, a qualification with which I most heartily agree after years of strenuous effort to abolish it from my wild garden. (p. 172)

Photo by Dr. Paul Bartsch

SENSITIVE FERN

Onoclea sensibilis

It looks rather attractive in the picture, and in broad masses in the wild, wet places, but after sufficient and patient trials I do not recommend the Sensitive Fern as a desirable in the wild garden. It is just another impudent marauder, like the Bracken and the Hay-scented Fern.

In some ancient tome Clute found this fern named "Dragon's Bridges," and it is sometimes called "Oak Fern" or "Oak-leaved Fern." (p. 174)

Photo by Dr. H. S. Barber

OSTRICH FERN

Pteretis nodulosa

The Ostrich Fern is at its best in the wet, sandy soil of half-shaded shores where its fronds often stand six feet high or more.

It is sometimes descriptively called the Shuttlecock Fern in Europe, but the popularity of the name Ostrich Fern has never been threatened. The botanical name, however, has been changed several times as will be seen from the list of botanical synonyms following the detailed fern descriptions. (p. 176)

Photo by Dr. E. T. Wherry

ROYAL FERN

Osmunda regalis

The delicate pinks and pale yellows of the uncoiling fronds of the Royal Fern are unequaled in beauty, save by the autumn tints of the Sassafras.

This fern has been known by numerous common names, the best of them suggested by its regal habit and aspect, such as Royal Osmund, King Fern, Regal Fern and Royal Moonwort. (p. 178)

Photo by Dr. C. R. Shoemaker

INTERRUPTED FERN

Osmunda claytoniana

The Interrupted Fern frequently wanders down a wooded slope nearly to the edge of a swamp, where the Royal and Cinnamon ferns are reveling in the placid water, but it never shows any disposition to join them and get its feet actually wet.

It is an excellent subject and widely used for foundation planting, and is not at all difficult to grow. It is sometimes called "Clayton's Fern" but "Interrupted" is a much better name. (p. 180)

Photo by Dr. C. R. Shoemaker

CINNAMON FERN

Osmunda cinnamomea

The crown of the rootstock of this fern is eaten by many country people who say it is tender, crisp and very palatable, tasting like raw cabbage. It is known in Europe as the "Heart of Osmond."

The botanical name *Osmunda* is supposed to have been suggested by the story of Osmund, the Water-man of Loch Tyne, who hid wife and child in a thicket of this fern when the Danes invaded Scotland. (p. 182)

Photo by Dr. H. S. Barber

COMMON GRAPE FERN

Botrychium dissectum var. *obliquum*

The so-called "Ternate" Grape fern, listed as a separate species in Gray's Botany, 7th Edition, is so like the above that it suggests a distinction without a difference. In fact Standardized Plant Names gives it as identical with the other, and so do several distinguished botanists. Perhaps there is another species that may be so named.

The Grape Ferns and Common Rattlesnake Ferns are not uncommon but are generally overlooked in rambles through the woods. (p. 184)

Photo by Dr. Paul Bartsch

CUT-LEAVED GRAPE FERN

Botrychium dissectum var. *typicum*

In Gray's Botany, 7th Edition, and most of the popular fern books, the Cut-leaved Grape Fern is classed as a mere variety of the ordinary Grape Fern. Recent and wider study, however, seems to indicate that the shoe is on the other foot and that the Cutleaf form is the true species and the other the variety. (p. 186)

Photo by Dr. E. T. Wherry

RATTLESNAKE FERN

Botrychium virginianum

The botanical generic name *Botrychium* is from the Greek, and means a cluster of grapes, in allusion to the shape and grouping of the sporecases. There are twenty-five or more species in this genus, widely scattered throughout the world.

Dr. Wherry tells me that the mountaineers of the southern Alleghanies call this the Indicator Fern because it is thought to indicate the location of valuable plants, especially Ginseng and Golden Seal. (p. 188)

Photo by Dr. C. R. Shoemaker

SHINING CLUB MOSS

Lycopodium lucidulum

One of the commonest of the Fern Allies known as Club Mosses, is the species shown above. It is usually a dweller in hemlock woods and differs from the three other species here described by producing its spores in the axils of its leaves instead of on "clubs." Some botanical authorities, because of this difference, say that it is not a club moss at all, and that "Staghorn Moss" would be a more fitting common name.

Photo by Dr. E. T. Wherry

RUNNING PINE

Lycopodium clavatum

Perhaps the most beautiful of the Club Mosses is the Running Pine, with its long stems creeping over the ground often for yards. Its color is a very vivid green and its suitability for festoons and drapery cause it to be in great demand for Christmas wreaths and hangings. However, in the interests of conservation Lycopodiums should not be gathered at all since they are becoming rare. A popular name for this species in some parts of the country is Snakemoss, which has the merit of being more suggestive than the accepted name.

Photo by Dr. C. R. Shoemaker

FLAT-BRANCH GROUND PINE

Lycopodium obscurum

The plants of the Ground Pine rather strikingly resembl miniature evergreen trees. I have frequently found them growing in large colonies, intertwined with the Running Pin and the Ground Pine and forming a rich green carpet tha covers extensive areas of the forest floor. The spores of thi and the preceding species furnish the Lycopodium powde used for flashlights, and for the relief of chafing. It is highl inflammable when dry.

Photo by Dr. E. L. Crandall

GROUND PINE

Locopodium complanatum

The Ground Pine is always one of the four most abundant and conspicuous club mosses of the eastern forests. Ground Pines are most frequently used for winter decorations. This practice should be discontinued and the plants spared from extermination. To a lesser extent than the others it yields Lycopodium powder.

There are over 100 species of club mosses known, of which 17 are native in the United States. The Resurrection Plant of Mexico is a near relative, belonging to the Selaginella group.

HOW TO IDENTIFY THE FERNS

Distinguishing Characteristics and Outline Illustrations of the 50 most conspicuous species of Eastern America.

1. Common Polypody

Polypòdium virginiánum

Fronds:—Three to ten inches long, occasionally longer; deeply divided into long, narrow usually obtuse segments; evergreen.

Fruit-dots:—Large, yellow-brown, roundish, and located midway between the *midvein* and margin of the segments.

Rootstocks:—Creeping along or just below the surface and branching freely.

Habitat:—Found most frequently on shaded rocks in moderately dry leaf-mold, where it generally forms dense, widely spreading mats of foliage. Also grows occasionally on tree trunks, and fallen logs.

Range:—From Alabama to the far North, and from Maine westward across the continent.

Distinguishing Mark:—The conspicuously prominent *fruit-dots.*

This fern has been given an unusual number of local common names. In Maine it is known among the natives as the Rock-cap Fern, a rather good descriptive name. In other sections it is called Stone Fern, Stone Brake, Moss Fern, Addler's Fern, Snake Fern, etc. It has been known in England for centuries as Common Polypody, and its favorite habitat over there is on trees.

Until recently the Polypody of Eastern America was supposed to be identical with the English species, but it is now considered distinct and has been given a different botanical name. The Polypody of the Colorado Rockies is, however, the same as the one that grows in England.

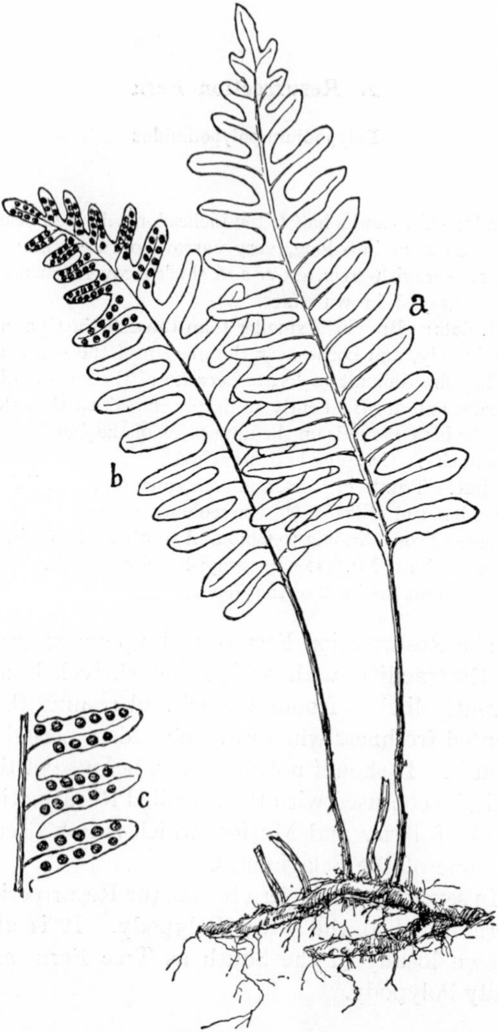

COMMON POLYPODY

a. Sterile Frond; b. Fertile Frond; c. Fruiting Segment.

2. Resurrection Fern

Polypòdium polypodioìdes

Fronds:—Two and a half to ten inches long, divided nearly to the stem into long, very narrow, obtuse segments.
Color:—Grayish-green above and thickly covered beneath with grayish-brown scales.
Fruit-dots:—Brownish, smaller than those of the Common Polypody, and borne near the margin of the segments. They are difficult to locate because of the surrounding scales and are frequently so deeply imbedded that they make little mounds on the upper side of the *frond.*
Rootstocks:—Creeping and branched.
Habitat:—Trunks of trees, and sometimes on rocks if there is a handful of leaf-mold convenient.
Range:—From Virginia to Ohio and south to the Gulf.
Distinguishing Marks:—Its grayish color and the scaly coating on the back of the *fronds.*

The Resurrection Fern owes its popular name to the facility with which the shriveled, apparently lifeless fronds uncurl and resume their wonted freshness when rain succeeds a period of drouth. It should not, however, because of this trait, be confused with the so-called Resurrection plant of Texas and Mexico, which is not a fern, but one of the Selaginellas.

In several popular fern books, the Resurrection Fern is called the Gray Polypody. It is also known locally in the South as Tree Fern, and Scaly Polypody.

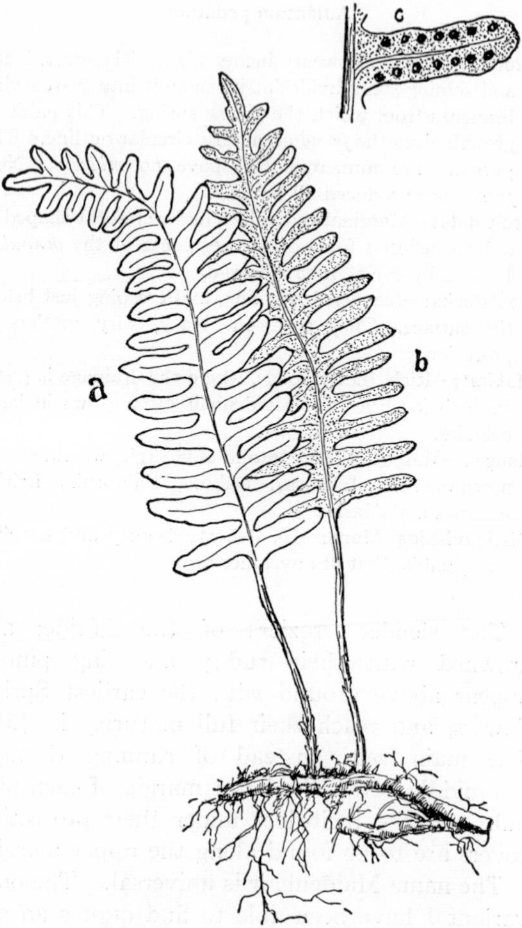

RESURRECTION FERN

a. Sterile Frond; b. Fertile Frond; c. Fruiting Segment.

3. Maidenhair Fern

Adiántum pedàtum

Fronds:—Eight to twenty inches high. The erect, black and shining stem divides at its summit into two curving branches from which the *pinnæ* spring. This habit of growth gives the *frond* an almost circular outline. The *pinnules* are numerous and have no *midvein.* New *fronds* are produced all Summer.

Fruit-dots:—Marginal and hidden under crescent-shaped or oblong reflexed folds of the segments of the *pinnules.* Practically every *frond* is fertile.

Rootstocks:—Slender, branching, and creeping just below the surface. They send out black, wiry rootlets in profusion.

Habitat:—Rich, moist woods, where the drainage is good. In such localities the Maidenhair often grows in large colonies.

Range:—Maine to the mountains of Georgia, westward and northward to Arkansas, Dakota, California, British America and Alaska.

Distinguishing Mark:—Its delicate beauty and peculiar form, unlike that of any other fern.

The slender croziers of the Maidenhair, crowned with their ruddy uncoiling pinnæ, appear above ground with the earliest Spring flowers, and reach their full maturity in July. The main vein, instead of running through the middle, forms the lower margin of each pinnule and the fruit-dots under their protecting covers are to be found along the upper margin.

The name Maidenhair is universal. The only variant I have been able to find quotes an old English book as calling it "The Foot-shaped Canadian Maidenhair," an evident reference to our American species.

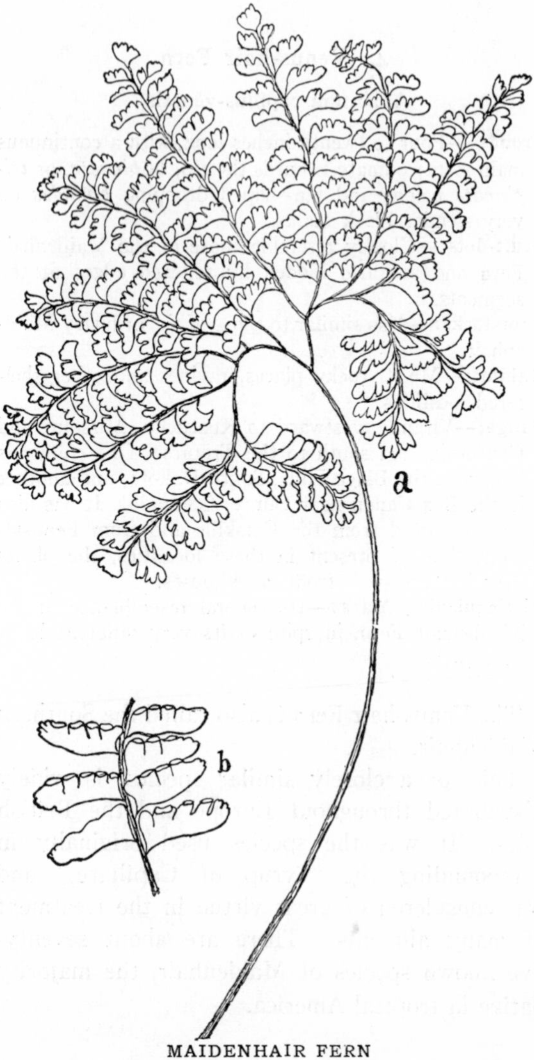

MAIDENHAIR FERN
a. Ordinary Frond; b. Fruiting Pinnules.

4. Venus-hair Fern

Adiántum capíllus-véneris

Fronds:—Four to twenty inches long, with a continuous main stem; pinnate towards the tip, *bi-pinnate*, or *tri-pinnate* below, and fan-shaped drooping *pinnules* on very slender black stalks.

Fruit-dots:—Closely resemble those of the Maidenhair Fern and are also hidden by reflexed edges of the segments.

Rootstocks:—Also similar to those of the ordinary Maidenhair.

Habitat:—Moist, rocky places, ravines and other sheltered localities.

Range:—Virginia westward to Kentucky, Missouri and California, and south to the Tropics. One colony is known in the Black Hills, South Dakota, and another in the Box Canon near Ouray, Colorado. It has also been reported from the Catskills and from Pennsylvania, but, if present in these localities, the plants may be "escapes" from greenhouses.

Distinguishing Mark:—Its general resemblance to the Maidenhair Fern, in spite of its very different habit of growth.

The Venus-hair Fern is also called the Southern Maidenhair.

This, or a closely similar species, is widely distributed throughout Europe and the British Isles. It was the species used originally in compounding the "Syrup of Capillare," and was considered of great virtue in the treatment of many ailments. There are about seventy-five known species of Maidenhair, the majority native in tropical America.

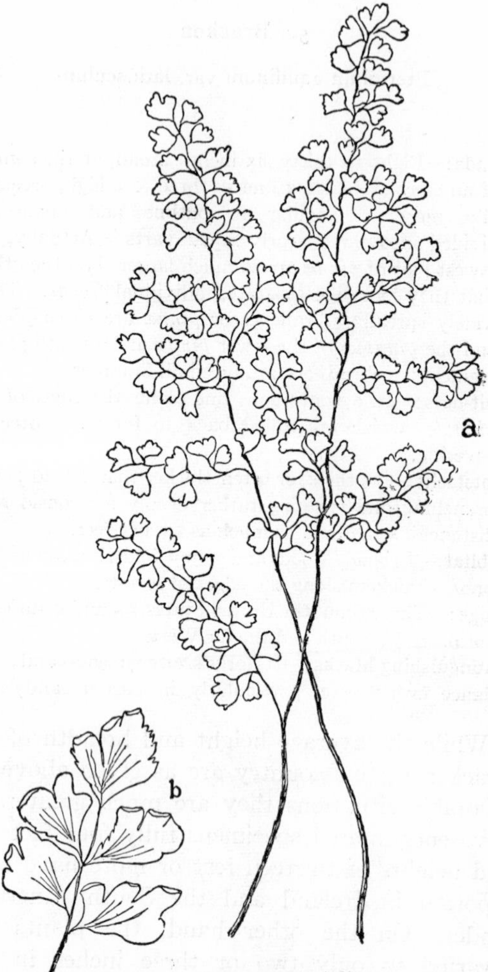

VENUS-HAIR FERN

a. Ordinary Frond; b. Fruiting Pinnules.

5. Bracken

Pterídium aquilinum var. latiúsculum

Fronds:—Eight to thirty-six inches broad, at the summit of an erect stout stalk one to three feet high, occasionally more. Triangular in outline and apparently divided into three nearly equal parts. Actually, the lowest pair of *pinnæ* are so much larger than the others that they look like separate, individual *fronds*. These widely spreading branches or *pinnæ* are twice *pinnate* and the *pinnules* of the lower *pinnæ* are cut into partial segments. *Fronds* are produced all Summer.

Fruit-dots:—In a continuous line along the edges of the *pinnules* which are rolled back to form a protective covering.

Rootstocks:—As thick, or often thicker than a lead pencil, branching and creeping rather deeply for considerable distances, sometimes as much as twenty feet.

Habitat:—In shady woods and sunny fields, but apparently prefers thickets along the edges of forests.

Range:—Throughout the United States, assuming different forms in the South and the far West.

Distinguishing Marks:—Its large size, coarseness and abundance everywhere, particularly in barren sandy soil.

While the average height and breadth of the Bracken in this country are as given above, in favorable situations they are much greater. I have encountered specimens fully four feet tall and heights of thirteen feet or more have been reported in Ireland and the South American Andes. On the other hand, the plants are dwarfed to only two or three inches in the far North. Also known as Brake, Eagle Fern, Turkey-foot Fern, and Umbrella Fern.

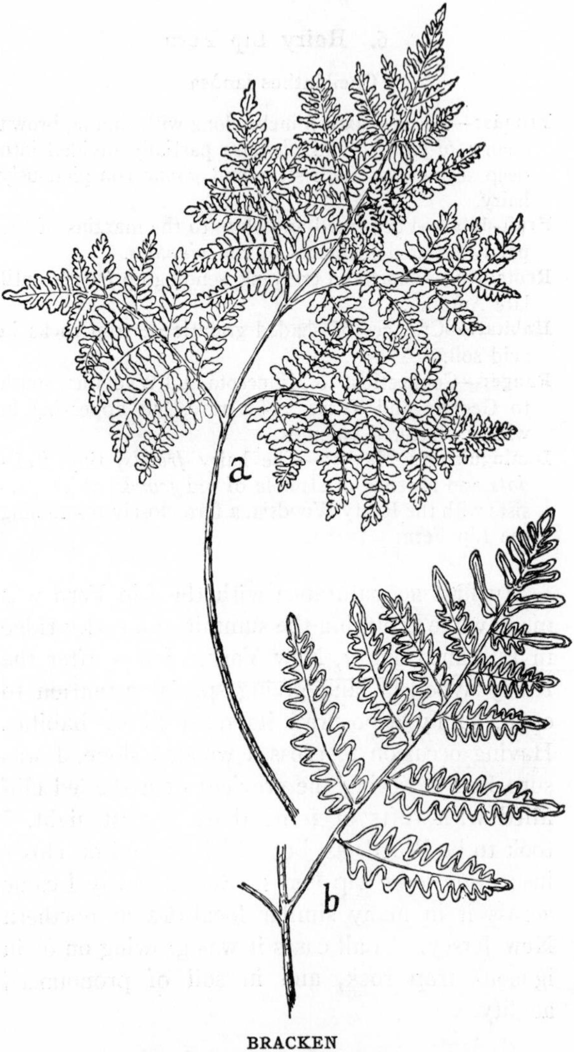

BRACKEN

a. Sterile Frond; b. Fruiting Pinna.

6. Hairy Lip Fern

Cheilánthes lanòsa

Fronds:—Four to sixteen inches long with shining brown stems; *bi-pinnate* and *pinnules* partially divided into deep segments. Both stem and *pinnæ* conspicuously hairy.

Fruit-dots:—Very small and close to the margins of the partly reflexed segments of the *pinnules.*

Rootstock:—Short and creeping, sending up *fronds* until late Autumn.

Habitat:—Crevices of shaded granitic or trap rocks in acid soil.

Range:—Connecticut to Minnesota and Wyoming, south to Georgia and Texas. Not rare, but appearing in widely scattered colonies.

Distinguishing Marks:—The hairy *fronds,* tiny *fruit-dots* and absence of stubble of old *fronds* which persists with the Rusty Woodsia, a fern closely resembling the Lip Fern.

My first acquaintance with the Lip Fern was made while exploring the summit of a rocky ridge in Putnam County, New York. I was after the Rusty Woodsia, and giving special attention to open, sunny exposures, its most likely habitat. Having occasion to cross a wooded slope, I was surprised at seeing the crevices of a shaded cliff filled with tufts of ferns that, at first sight, I took to be Woodsias, but which proved on closer inspection to be Lip Ferns. Subsequently I came across it in many similar localities in northern New Jersey. In all cases it was growing on or in igneous trap rock, and in soil of pronounced acidity.

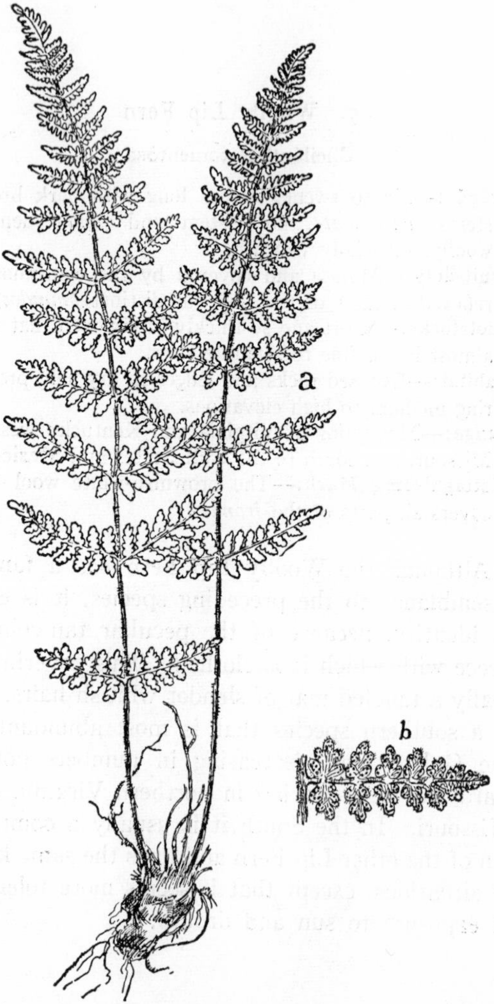

HAIRY LIP FERN

a. Ordinary Fronds; b. Fruiting Pinnules.

7. Woolly Lip Fern

Cheilánthes tomentòsa

Fronds:—Six to twenty inches long with dark brown stems, *tri-pinnate,* both stem and *pinnæ* densely woolly, especially beneath.

Fruit-dots:—Minute and covered by the continuously reflexed margins of the tiny but distinct *pinnules.*

Rootstocks:—Short and so thickly interwoven that it is almost impossible to separate them.

Habitat:—Exposed rocks and ledges in dry soil, preferring medium to high elevations.

Range:—Mountains of Virginia and Kentucky west to Missouri and south to the Gulf States and Mexico.

Distinguishing Mark:—The brownish-white wool that covers all parts of the *fronds.*

Although the Woolly Lip Fern has a family resemblance to the preceding species, it is easy to identify, because of the peculiar tan-colored fleece with which it is clothed. This covering is really a tangled mat of slender whitish hairs. It is a southern species that is most abundant in the Gulf States, decreasing in numbers northward and disappearing in northern Virginia and Missouri. In the South it is usually a companion of the other Lip Fern and likes the same kind of situations, except that it seems more tolerant of exposure to sun and drouth.

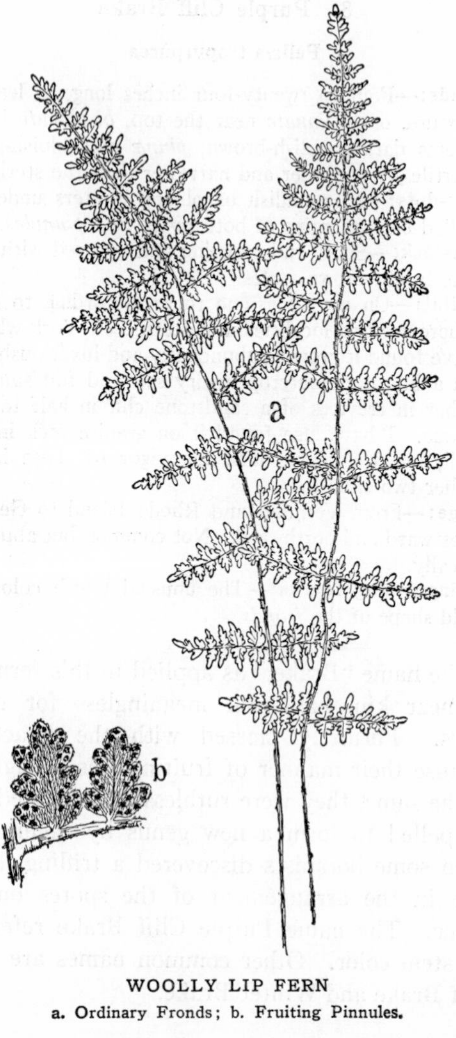

WOOLLY LIP FERN
a. Ordinary Fronds; b. Fruiting Pinnules.

8. Purple Cliff Brake

Pellæa tropurpùrea

Fronds:—Four to twenty-four inches long, of leathery texture, once *pinnate* near the top, *bi-pinnate* below. Stems dark purplish-brown, *pinnæ* pale bluish-green. Fertile *fronds* taller and narrower than the sterile.

Fruit-dots:—In roundish or oblong clusters under the rolled back margins of both *pinnæ* and *pinnules*.

Rootstock:—Short and creeping and covered with hair-like bright brown scales.

Habitat:—On dry limestone rocks, according to Gray. There are two localities in eastern New York where I have found it growing abundantly and luxuriously, one on a limestone outcrop in dry soil and full sun—the other in crevices of a sandstone cliff in half to deep shade. I have also found it on granite rock in acid soil, but the plants lack the vigor of those in the other two situations.

Range:—From Vermont and Rhode Island to Georgia, westward and northward. Not common but abundant locally.

Distinguishing Marks:—The unusual bluish color and odd shape of the *fronds*.

The name "Brake," as applied to this fern and its near kin, has been meaningless for many years. Formerly classed with the Brackens, because their manner of fruiting was thought to be the same, they were ruthlessly kidnapped and compelled to form a new genus by themselves, when some botanists discovered a trifling difference in the arrangement of the spores on the pinnæ. The name Purple Cliff Brake refers to the stem color. Other common names are Blue Cliff Brake and Winter Brake.

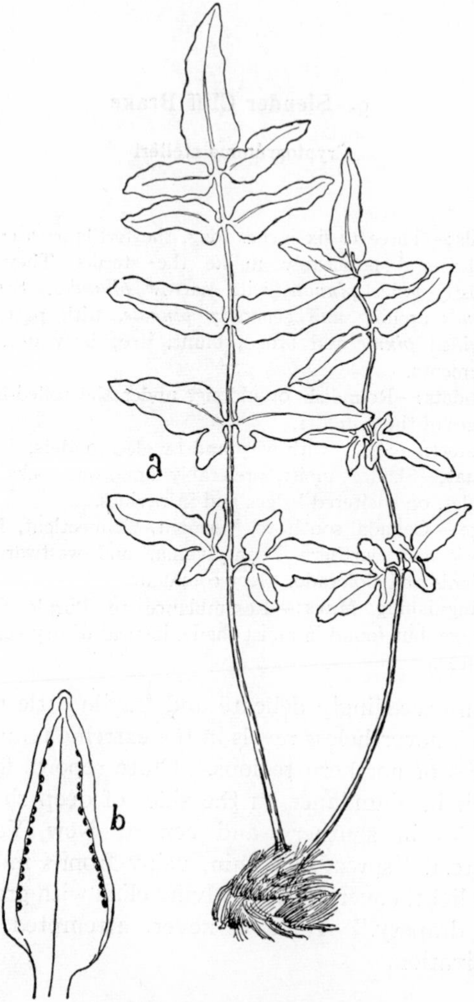

PURPLE CLIFF BRAKE
a. Ordinary Fronds; b. Fruiting Pinnule.

9. Slender Cliff Brake

Cryptográmma stellèri

Fronds:—Three to six inches long, the fertile ones erect, taller and noticeably unlike the sterile. They are mostly twice *pinnate*, with narrow *pinnules*. Sterile *fronds* arching and generally *pinnate*, with partially divided *pinnæ* and broad, blunt, irregularly notched segments.

Fruit-dots:—Roundish or oblong, under the rolled-back edges of the *pinnules*.

Rootstock:—Short, with wiry and tangled rootlets.

Habitat:—Shaded, moist, preferably limestone rocks and shales, on sheltered ledges and in ravines.

Range:—Canada south to Vermont, Connecticut, New York and northern Pennsylvania, and westward to Illinois and Colorado. Not common.

Distinguishing Mark:—Resemblance to Purple Cliff Brake, but found in moist shade, instead of dry sunny places.

An exceedingly delicate and fragile little fern which nevertheless revels in the extreme temperatures of northern regions. Clute reports finding it in abundance on the sides of deep shady ravines in southern and central New York, where it "spreads its thin, veiny fronds in the dim light, covering the shelving cliffs with graceful drapery." I have never attempted its cultivation.

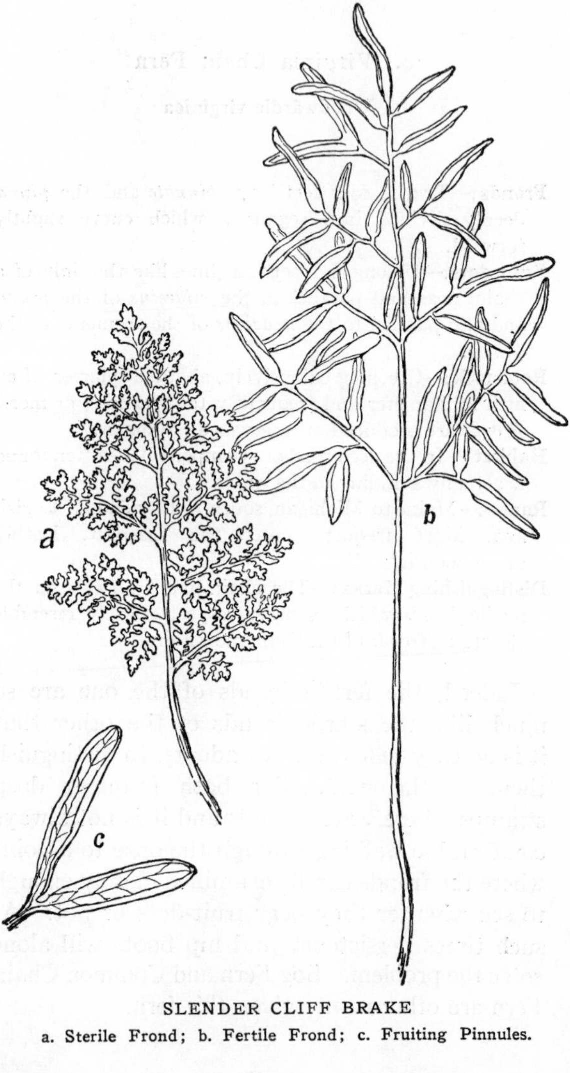

SLENDER CLIFF BRAKE

a. Sterile Frond; b. Fertile Frond; c. Fruiting Pinnules.

10. Virginia Chain Fern

Woodwárdia virgínica

Fronds:—Two to four feet long, *pinnate* and the *pinnæ* deeply divided into segments which curve slightly forward.

Fruit-dots:—Oblong and borne in lines like the links of a chain, near and parallel to the *midveins* of the *pinnæ* and also parallel to the *midveins* of the segments of the *pinnæ*.

Rootstock:—Creeping extensively, about a quarter of an inch in diameter and frequently ten feet long or more. *Fronds* are produced at intervals all Summer.

Habitat:—In the deep mud of swamps; I have often found it actually standing in the water.

Range:—Maine to Michigan, south to Florida and Louisiana. Most frequent near the seacoast. Rather uncommon inland.

Distinguishing Marks:—The chain-like *fruit-dots* on the fertile *fronds* which in other respects closely resemble the sterile *fronds* of the Cinnamon Fern.

Indeed, the fertile fronds of the one are so much like the sterile fronds of the other that it is no easy task, even for adepts, to distinguish them in the wild. For both frequent deep swamps where water stands and it is not always comfortable walking through the ooze to a point where the fronds can be examined closely enough to see whether they bear fruit-dots or not. At such times persistency and hip boots will alone solve the problem. Bog Fern and Common Chain Fern are other names given this fern.

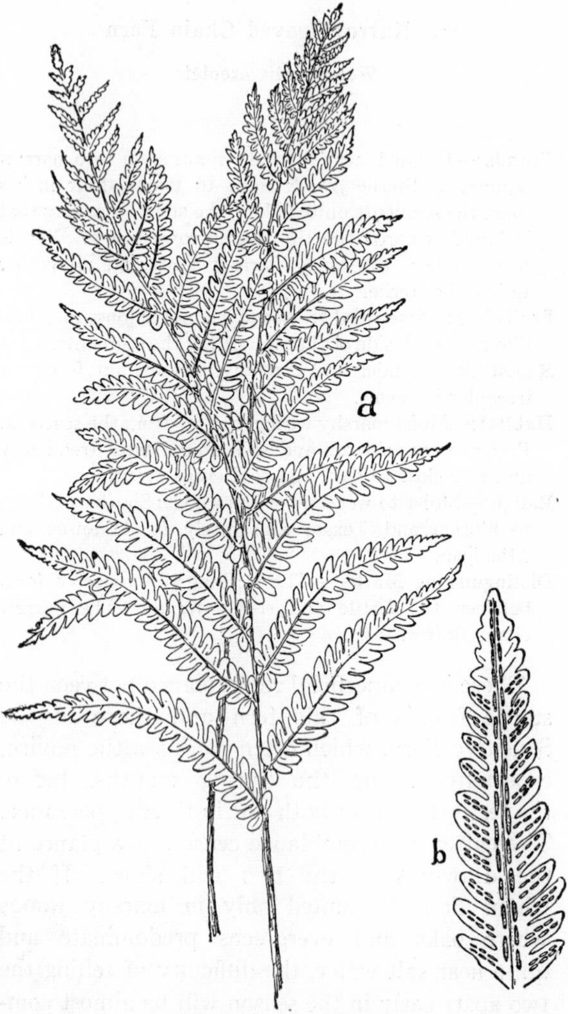

VIRGINIA CHAIN FERN
a. Ordinary Fronds; b. Fruiting Pinna.

11. Narrow-leaved Chain Fern

Woodwárdia areolàta

Fronds:—Divided nearly to the main stem into narrow segments. Sterile *fronds* eight to twenty-four inches long, the segments united along the stem by a wing that is broad towards the tip but narrows below. Fertile *fronds* taller, with very narrow segments; altogether unlike the sterile.

Fruit-dots:—One-third to two-fifths inches long, in chain-like rows each side of the *midveins* of the segments.

Rootstock:—Slender and creeping, sending up *fronds* at irregular intervals.

Habitat:—Moist marshy woods, not far from the seacoast. Prefers very acid soil and so is found most frequently under or close to oaks and coniferous evergreens.

Range:—Moist to wet acid soil in woods; Southern Maine to Florida and Texas: also rarely in Arkansas and Michigan.

Distinguishing Marks:—The striking difference of form between the fertile and sterile *fronds*. The narrow chain-like *fruit-dots*.

There is a superficial resemblance between the sterile fronds of this fern and those of the Sensitive Fern, which often confuses the novice, especially during the Spring months, before the fertile fronds of both put in their appearance. Thereafter all resemblance ceases, as a glance at the drawings of the two will show. If the Chain Fern is hunted only in marshy woods where oaks and evergreens predominate and quite near salt water, the difficulty of telling the two apart early in the season will be almost completely obviated. Net-veined Chain Fern and Dwarf Chain Fern are other common names for this fern.

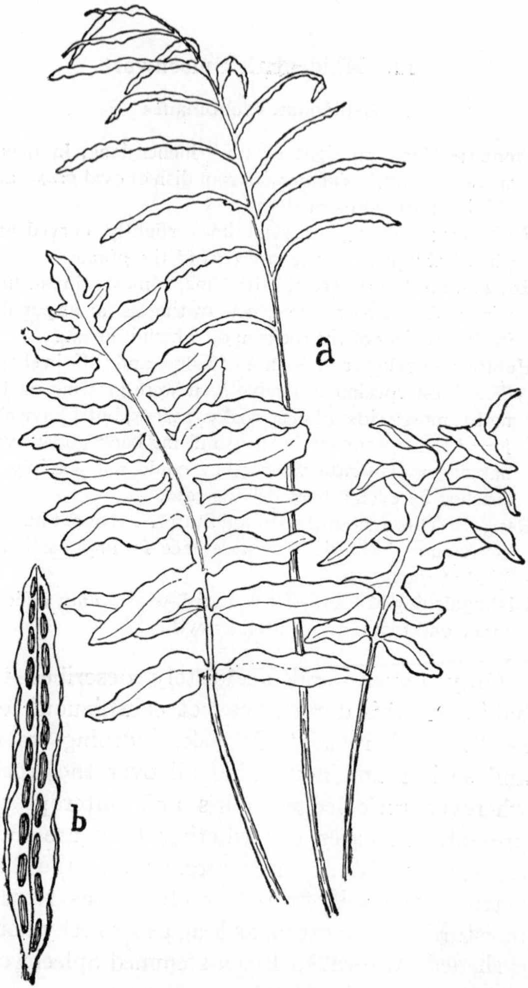

NARROW-LEAVED CHAIN FERN
a. Fertile Fornd; b. Fruiting Pinna.

12. Maidenhair Spleenwort

Asplènium trichómanes

Fronds:—Three to eight or nine inches long, in dense, spreading tufts; *pinnate* with roundish or oval *pinnæ* and shining purple-brown stems.

Fruit-dots:—Oblong or sometimes slightly curved and placed obliquely to the *midveins* of the *pinnæ*.

Rootstock:—Short, erect, with fine, almost thread-like, wiry and matted rootlets, penetrating as far as possible in the crevices of the rocks upon which it grows.

Habitat:—Pockets and fissures of ledges and cliffs in shade. The finest specimens I have seen were growing on the moist, mossy sides of deep rocky ravines, but I have also found fine specimens in dry sand far back under overhanging rock strata where they could not possibly be reached by even a hard driving rain.

Range:—Throughout the United States. Frequent but not common and showing no preference for any particular kind of rock.

Distinguishing Marks:—Its roundish-oval *pinnæ*, delicate grace and distinctive tufted growth.

Gray tersely and accurately describes the habitat of this diminutive yet conspicuous fern as "shaded rocks." It asks nothing more, and so is found flourishing all over the world, wherever rock ledges, cliffs and outcrops are present. It cares not whether they are limestone, or sandstone, or granite, or what the character of the soil, or the conditions as regards moisture and exposure, as long as its rocky home is shaded. Also called Black-stemmed Spleenwort and Wall Spleenwort.

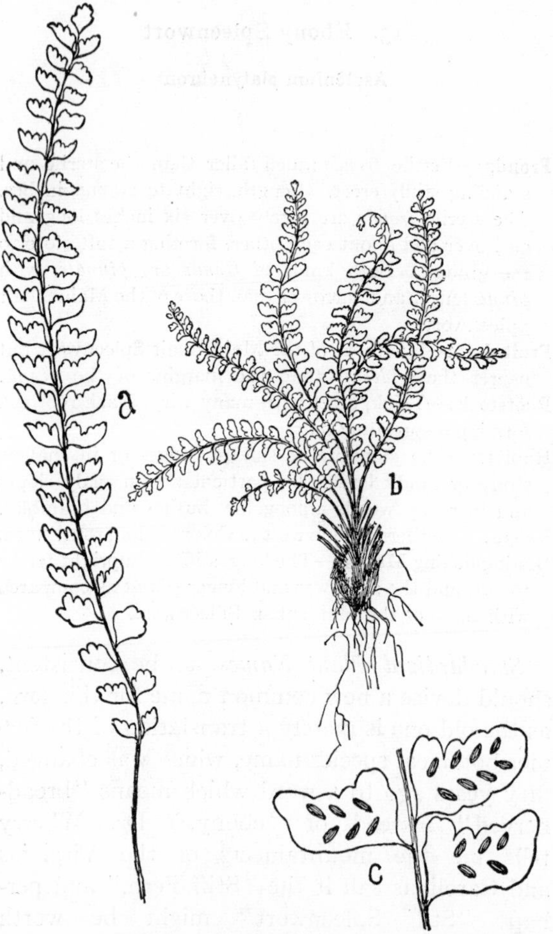

MAIDENHAIR SPLEENWORT

a. Single Frond; b. An average plant; c. Fruiting Pinnæ.

13. Ebony Spleenwort

Asplènium platyneùron

Fronds:—Fertile *fronds* much taller than the sterile and standing stiffly erect. Length, eight to twenty inches. The sterile *fronds* are rarely over six inches long and curl over and about each other, forming a tuft close to the ground. Both kinds of *fronds* are *pinnate*, with *pinnæ* longer and narrower than those of the Maidenhair Spleenwort.

Fruit-dots:—like those of the Maidenhair Spleenwort but nearer the *midveins* than the margins of the *pinnæ*.

Rootstock:—Thick, erect with many wiry, black rootlets, forming a spreading mat.

Habitat:—The summits of shaded ledges or in shallow stony or sandy leaf-mold, particularly on shaly slopes and in rocky woods among low bushes and brambles.

Range:—Southern Maine west to Colorado and southward.

Distinguishing Marks:—The long, stiff and upright fertile *fronds*, and the narrower and longer *pinnæ* as compared with those of the Maidenhair Spleenwort.

Standardized Plant Names, to be consistent, should devise a new common name for this fern, as the old one is merely a translation of the former botanical species-name, which was changed, fifty years ago to a word which means "broad-nerved" instead of "ebony." Dr. Wherry tells me the mountaineers of the Virginias and Carolinas call it the "Stiff Fern," and perhaps "Stiff Spleenwort" might be worth considering.

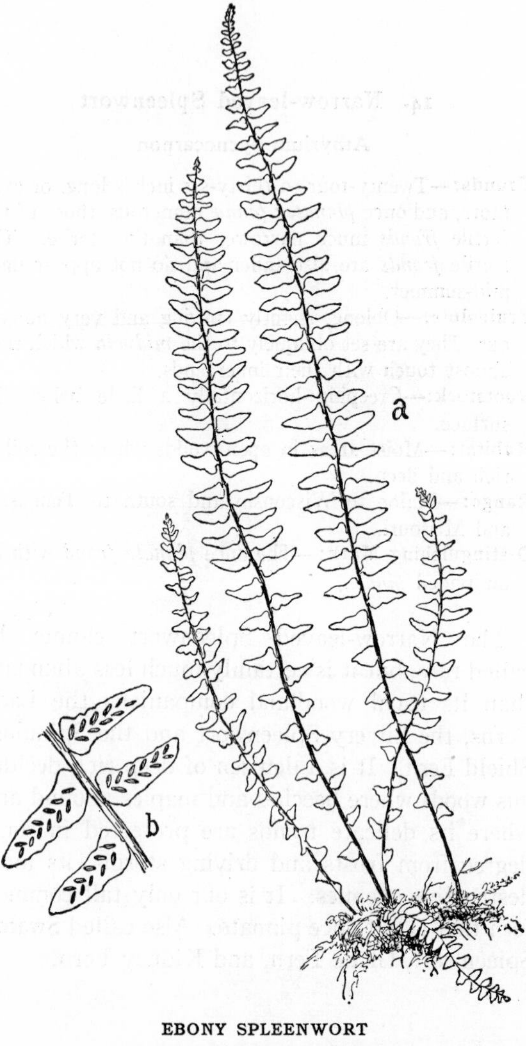

EBONY SPLEENWORT

a. Ordinary Fronds; b. Fruiting Pinnæ

14. Narrow-leaved Spleenwort

Athýrium pycnocarpon

Fronds:—Twenty-four to thirty-six inches long, or even more, and once *pinnate; pinnæ* numerous, those of the fertile *fronds* much narrower than the sterile. The sterile *fronds* are also taller and do not appear until mid-summer.

Fruit-dots:—Oblong, slightly curving and very numerous. They are set obliquely to the *midvein* which they almost touch with their inner ends.

Rootstock:—Creeping horizontally a little below the surface.

Habitat:—Moist areas in open woods where the soil is rich and deep.

Range:—Maine to Wisconsin and south to Tennessee and Missouri.

Distinguishing Mark:—The once *pinnate frond* with its undivided *pinnæ.*

The Narrow-leaved Spleenwort cannot be called rare, but it is certainly much less abundant than its usual woodland companions the Lady Ferns, the Silvery Spleenwort and the Spinulose Shield Fern. It is a denizen of deep rich deciduous woods where beeches and maples abound and where its delicate fronds are protected in some degree from frosts and driving storms, its most destructive enemies. It is our only tall common fern that is but once pinnate. Also called Swamp Spleenwort, Glade Fern, and Kidney Fern.

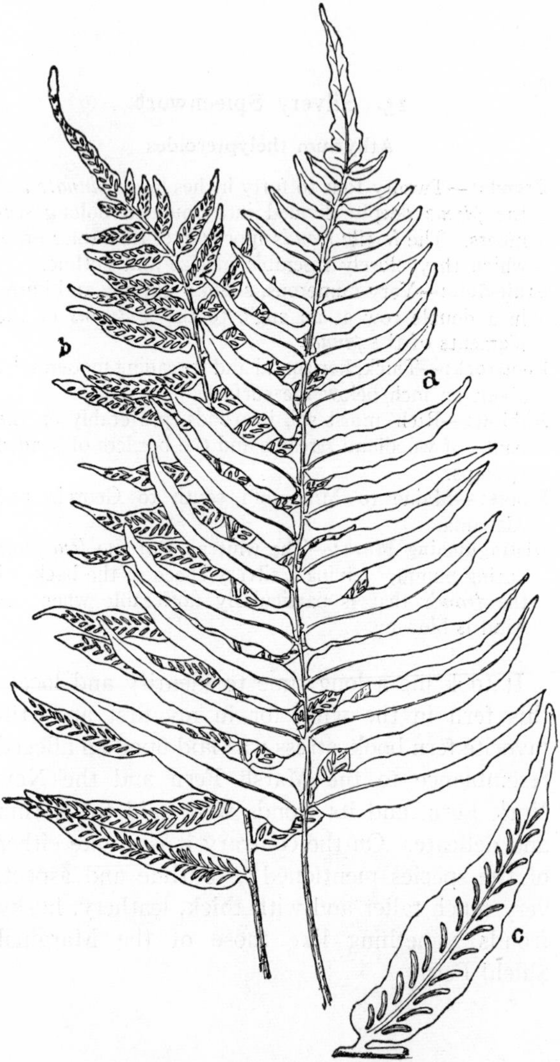

NARROW-LEAVED SPLEENWORT

a. Sterile Frond; b. Fertile Frond; c. Fruiting Pinnule.

15. Silvery Spleenwort

Athýrium thelypteroides

Fronds:—Twenty-four to forty inches long; *pinnate* and the *pinnæ* deeply divided into rounded oblong segments. The fertile *fronds* appear later than the sterile, which they closely resemble in size and outline.

Fruit-dots:—Very numerous, slightly curving and borne in a double row at an angle to the *midveins* of the segments of the *pinnæ*.

Rootstock:—Thick, horizontal and spreading moderately, about an inch below the surface.

Habitat:—Rich, moist soil in woods, proferably on the banks of woodland streams and the borders of shaded swamps.

Range:—Maine to Minnesota south to Georgia and Alabama.

Distinguishing Mark:—The whiteness of the *fruit-dots* during Summer, giving a silvery sheen to the backs of the *fronds* that is particularly noticeable when the wind is blowing.

It took me a long time to identify and locate this fern in the wild, for in my first and still favorite fern book, stress was laid upon an alleged resemblance to the Marsh Fern and the New York Fern, and its fronds were said to be thin and delicate. On the contrary it is unlike either of the species mentioned in outline and aspect, very much taller and with thick, leathery, husky fronds something like those of the Marginal Shield Fern.

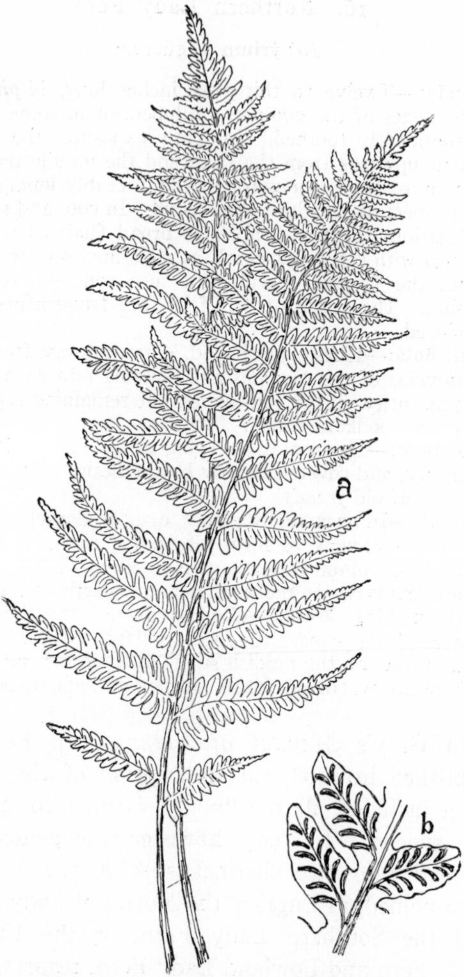

SILVERY SPLEENWORT

a. Ordinary Fronds; b. Fruiting Pinnules.

16. Northern Lady Fern

Athýrium angústum

Fronds:—Twelve to thirty-six inches long, *bi-pinnate,* the edges of the *pinnules* scalloped, or in some forms prominently toothed. In sunny exposures the *pinnæ* slant upwards from the stem and the middle pairs of the most conspicuous form are noticeably long, giving an aspect of breadth to the *frond.* In cool and shaded situations the *fronds* are also broad (half as wide as long) with the *pinnæ* nearly at right angles to the stem and the *pinnules* deeply cut into rounded, toothed lobes. The stems of this form are frequently wine-colored.

Fruit-dots:—Horseshoe-shaped, curving away from the *midveins* of the *pinnules* and merging into each other at maturity, in the sun-loving, but remaining separate in the woodland forms.

Rootstock:—Horizontal, creeping at or just under the surface, and covered thickly by the fleshy bases of the stems of old *fronds.*

Habitat:—In open sunny places, or cool, densely shaded woods according to form, preferring moist, rich soil.

Range:—Common throughout New England, New York and Pennsylvania, more abundant in northern sections.

Distinguishing Marks:—*Roots* covered by the stem bases of old *fronds*; the upward slant of the *pinnæ* in one form and the reddish stems in the other, although there are woodland forms without this characteristic.

In Gray's *Manual of Botany,* 7th Edition, published in 1908, the description of the Lady Fern included all the "many varying forms" in one species. In 1917, however, the genus was divided into two distinct species, which have been named, in English, the Northern Lady Fern, and the Southern Lady Fern, or the Upland Lady Fern and Lowland Lady Fern, respectively. Each species has absorbed its quota of the numerous variations.

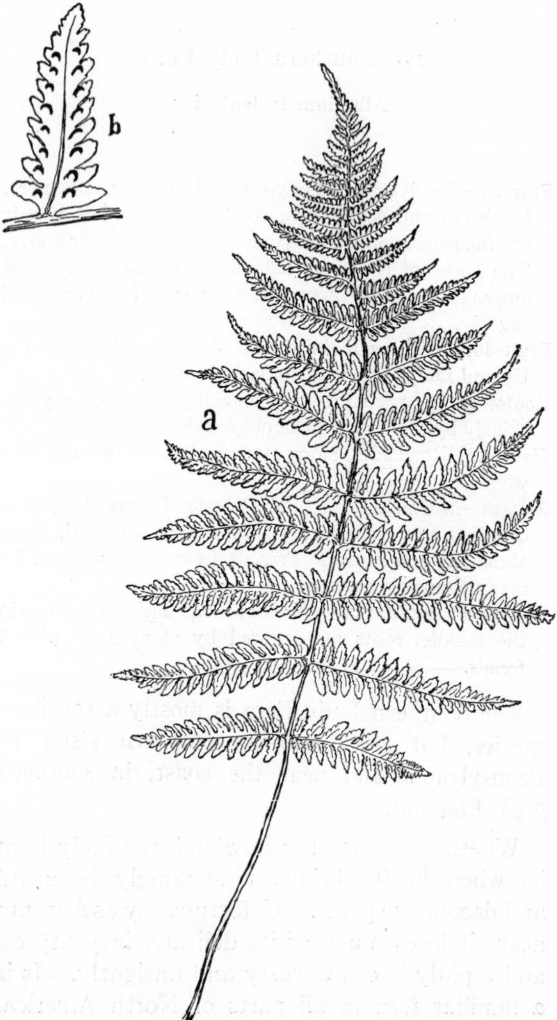

NORTHERN LADY FERN

a. Ordinary Frond; b. Fruiting Pinnule.

17. Southern Lady Fern

Athýrium asplenioìdes

Fronds:—Twelve to thirty-six inches long, or more, *bi-pinnate* and widest near the bottom, the lowest pair of *pinnæ* being only slightly shorter than the pair above. The *pinnæ* of the lower half of the *fronds* are at right angles to the stem, those of the upper half slant upward slightly.

Fruit-dots:—The same size and shape as those of the Upland Lady Fern and similarly located.

Rootstock:—Horizontal and creeping but *not* covered thickly by the remnants of old *fronds*.

Habitat:—Roadsides, along stone walls and in moist rich woods.

Range:—Massachusetts and Rhode Island to North Carolina and westward to Ohio and Missouri, more abundant southward. Present in one or more of its many forms throughout the country.

Distinguishing Marks:—*Fronds* as wide near the base as in the middle: roots *not* covered by stem bases of old *fronds*.

The Southern Lady Fern is mostly a southern species, but runs into its northern sister in Pennsylvania and near the coast, in southern New England.

Whether Highland or Lowland, the Lady Fern is, when in its prime, a strikingly beautiful and decorative plant. Unfortunately as Autumn nears it loses much of its delicate, lacy aspect, and rapidly becomes rusty and unsightly. It is a familiar fern in all parts of North America.

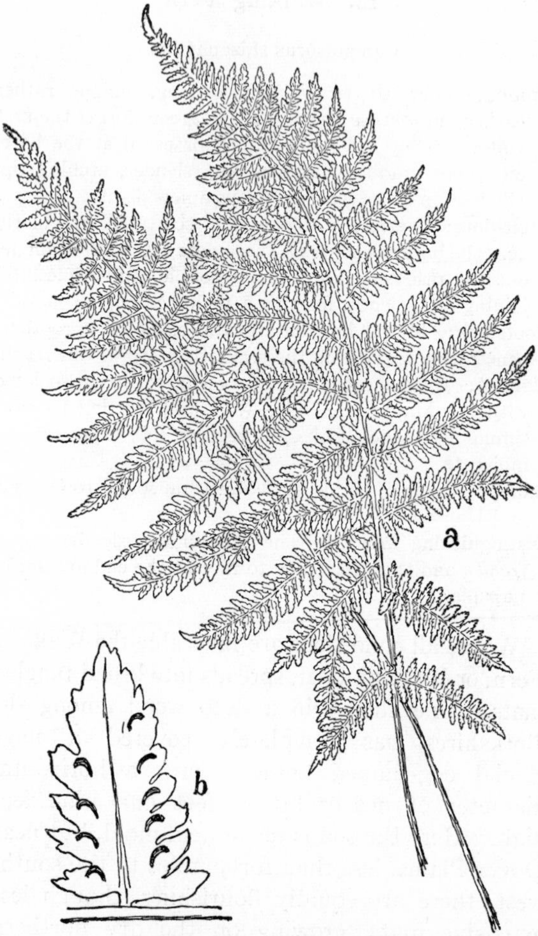

SOUTHERN LADY FERN

a. Ordinary Fronds; b. Fruiting Pinnule.

18. Walking Fern

Camptosòrus rhizophýllus

Fronds:—Four to twelve inches long, simple, rather leathery in texture and remaining green during the first winter. They are heart-shaped or eared at the base, and taper gradually into a long, slender, arching tip, which often takes root and forms a new plant.

Fruit-dots:—Narrowly oblong and scattered irregularly near the base of the *frond*, those near the *midvein* single, but the others inclined to be double, and sometimes joining at the ends, forming a V-shaped angle.

Rootstock:—Short, horizontal with black wiry rootlets, penetrating crevices in the rocks that are within reach.

Habitat:—Shaded rocks and mossy ledges: often associated with the Maidenhair Spleenwort and seeming to have similar likes and dislikes, as regards soil, exposure and moisture.

Range:—Central Maine to Minnesota, south to Georgia and Kansas.

Distinguishing Marks:—The undivided slender-tipped *fronds*, and their tendency to root at the end and make new plants.

Where all conditions are favorable the Walking Fern, or Walking Leaf, spreads into broad tangled mats. One colony in a deep wood among the Berkshires has completely covered a huge glacial egg-shaped boulder with a horizontal diameter of nearly fifteen feet and nine feet high. Here the soil is moist acid mold, but near Dover Plains, less than forty miles to the south-west, there are equally flourishing, though less extensive mats, growing on the dry northern slopes of limestone ledges, in pure lime sand.

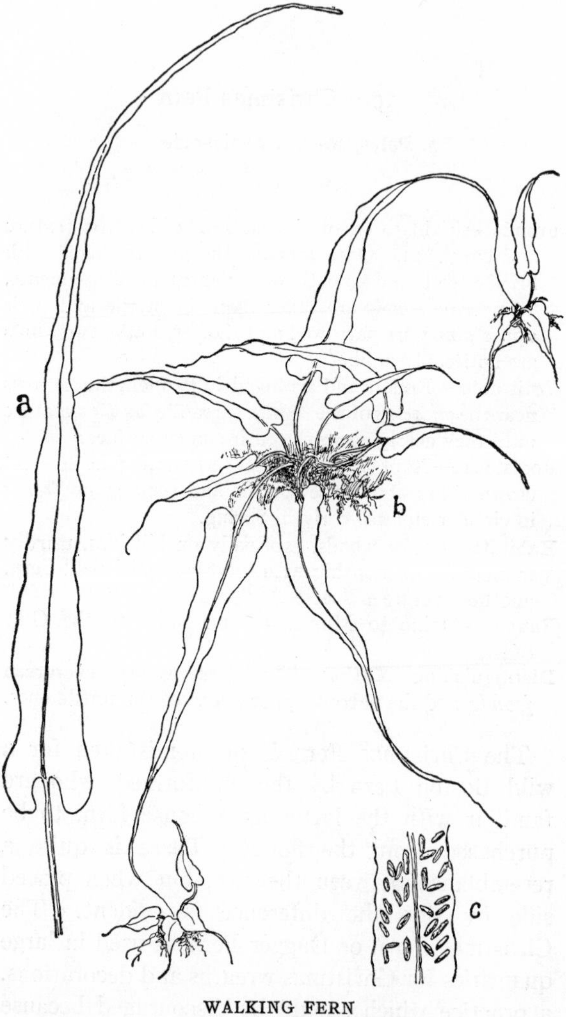

WALKING FERN

a. Simple Frond (undivided); b. average plant; c. Section of Fruiting or Fertile Frond.

19. Christmas Fern

Polýstìchum acrostichoìdes

Fronds:—Eight to twenty inches long, of leathery texture and evergreen. Once *pinnate*, the *pinnæ* fringed with bristly teeth and sometimes cut into partial segments. The fertile *fronds* are taller than the sterile and their upper *pinnæ* are narrowed and shorter, so the two kinds are noticeably unlike.

Fruit-dots:—Round and arranged in two lengthwise rows near the *midveins* of the *pinnæ*, spreading as they mature until they nearly cover the entire under surface.

Rootstock:—Stout and creeping, terminating in an erect crown rising above the surface and sending up *fronds* in circular clumps, early in Spring.

Habitat:—Rocky woods, especially on hillsides, usually in close companionship with the Marginal Shield Fern, another evergreen species.

Range:—Maine to Minnesota and south to the Gulf States.

Distinguishing Marks:—The dark, glossy evergreen *fronds,* and the narrow upper *pinnæ* of the fertile ones.

The Christmas Fern is often mistaken for a wild Boston Fern by the uninformed, who are familiar with the latter as a house fern, to be purchased from the florist. There is quite a resemblance between the two, but when placed side by side the difference is evident. The Christmas Fern, or Dagger Fern, is used in large quantities for Christmas wreaths and decorations, a practice which should be discouraged because commercial use of wild ferns is causing some species to become quite rare.

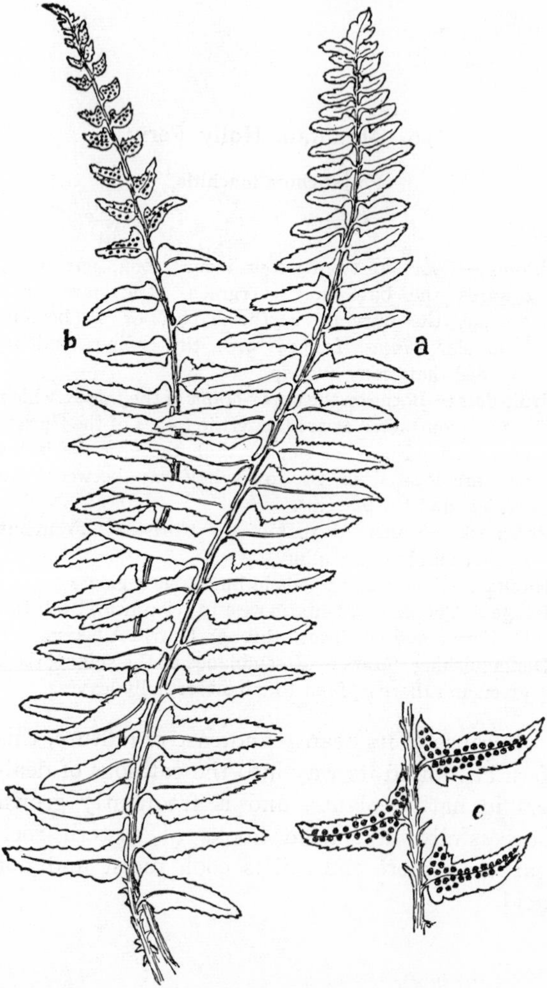

CHRISTMAS FERN
a. Sterile Frond; b. Fertile Frond; c. Fruiting Pinnæ.

20. Mountain Holly Fern

Polýstichum lonchìtis

Fronds:—Four to twenty-four inches long, narrowing towards the base and evergreen. They are once *pinnate*, the curving, scythe-shaped, or at bottom triangular *pinnæ*, fringed with tiny spines and so crowded that many overlap.

Fruit-dots:—Borne on the upper *pinnæ* of the *fronds*, which are not contracted as are the fertile *fronds* of the Christmas Fern. They are smaller than those of the latter and are located in two rows half-way between the *midvein* and the margins.

Rootstock:—Similar to that of the Christmas Fern but smaller and less spreading.

Habitat:—Cold rocky woods in limestone regions.

Range:—Quebec and Ontario west to Wisconsin, Utah and California and northward through British America.

Distinguishing Mark:—Resemblance of the shining dark green and thorny *pinnæ* to miniature holly leaves.

Because of its beauty and ease of culture, this fern has found its way into the catalogs of dealers in native plants, and is frequently grown successfully in shaded nooks of eastern rock gardens, where the soil is cool, moist and not acid.

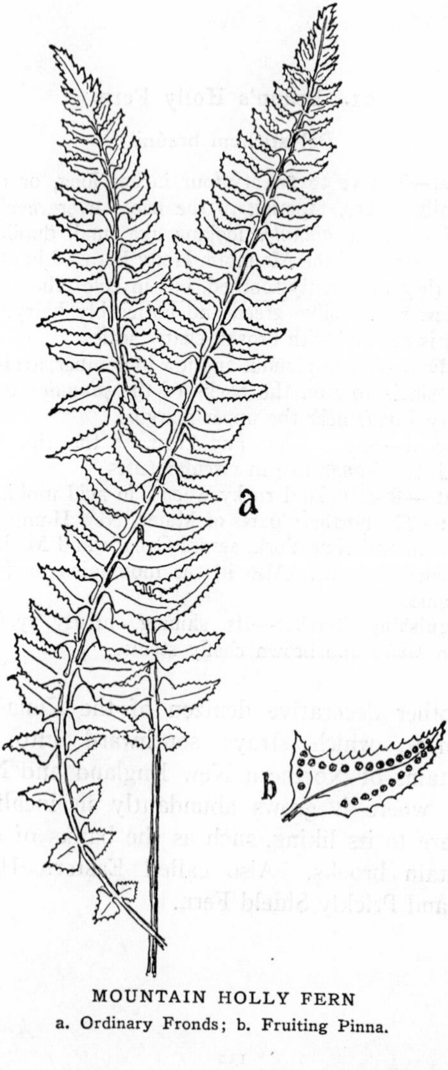

MOUNTAIN HOLLY FERN
a. Ordinary Fronds; b. Fruiting Pinna.

21. Braun's Holly Fern

Polýstichum braúnii

Fronds:—Twelve to twenty-four inches long, or occasionally longer, tapering to the base; evergreen and *bi-pinnate,* the *pinnules* looking like small duplicates of the *pinnæ* of the Mountain Holly Fern. Like them too, they are bristly-toothed, but in color they are a lighter, rather olive green and noticeably hairy. The stem is covered with brown, chaffy scales.

Fruit-dots:—Inconspicuous and few in number, arranged in a single row on the backs of the *pinnules* of ordinary *fronds* near the upper margins.

Rootstock:—Short, stout and erect at the tip, from which the *fronds* rise in circular tufts.

Habitat:—Rich upland rocky woods, in acid mold.

Range:—The northern parts of Maine, New Hampshire, Vermont and New York, across Canada and Michigan to Lake Superior. Also in the mountains of Pennsylvania.

Distinguishing Marks:—Its shining, bristly, yellow-green *pinnæ* and brown chaffy stems.

Another decorative denizen of the Canadian provinces, which strays southward into the mountains of Northern New England and New York, where it grows abundantly in localities that are to its liking, such as the banks of cold mountain brooks. Also called Eastern Holly Fern and Prickly Shield Fern.

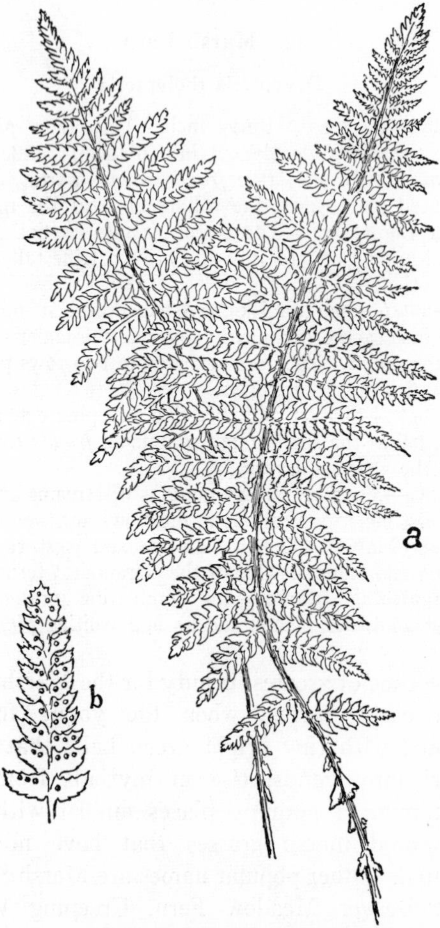

BRAUN'S HOLLY FERN

a. Ordinary Fronds; b. Fruiting Pinna.

22. Marsh Fern

Dryopteris thelypteris

Fronds:—Twelve to thirty inches long, once *pinnate*, and the *pinnæ* deeply cut into oblong, rounded segments which, on fertile *fronds* when in fruit, appear pointed, because of the rolling back of the margins over the *spores*. The fertile *fronds* do not appear until middle or late July and grow a trifle taller than the others.

Fruit-dots:—Small and kidney-shaped at first, but soon run into each other, nearly covering the under surface of the *pinnæ*. They are arranged in two rows parallel to and near the *midveins*.

Rootstock:—Slender and cord-like, creeping extensively just below the surface and producing *fronds* throughout the growing season.

Habitat:—Marshes, watery margins of streams and still waters, moist depressions in meadows and wet woods.

Range:—Maine to North Carolina and west to Oklahoma and Kansas. One of the commonest ferns.

Distinguishing Marks:—Its dominating presence in most wild, wet places, and its odd fruiting *pinnæ*.

The time of greatest beauty for the Marsh Fern is in early Spring, when the young fronds, crowned with tiny bright green balls that later uncurl into fronds, rise in myriads from the black mud of swampy places amidst withered, tan-colored marsh grasses that have not yet sprouted. Other popular names are Marsh Shield Fern, Beaver Meadow Fern, Creeping Water Fern, Quill Fern, and Snuff-box Fern.

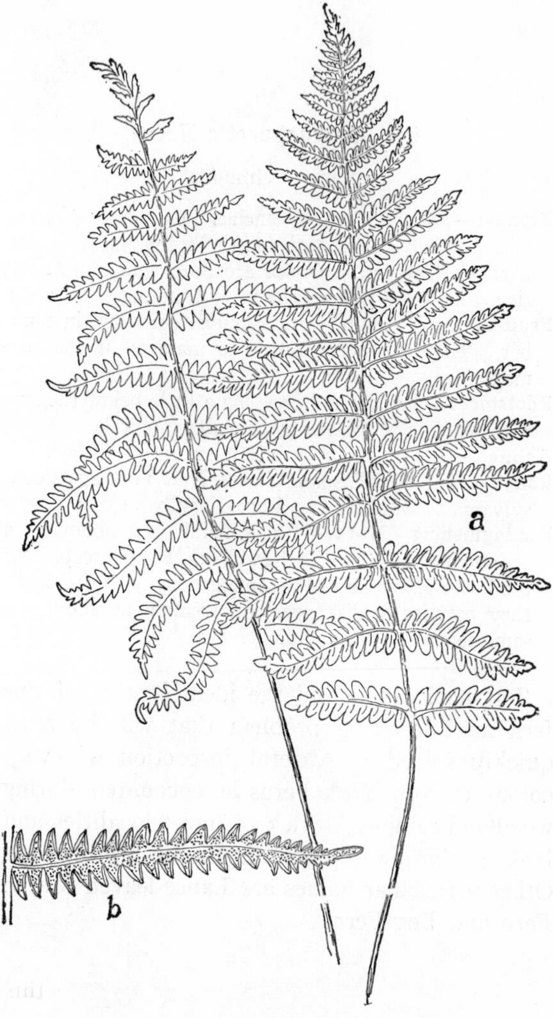

MARSH FERN

a. Sterile Frond; Fertile Frond not Lettered; b. Fruiting Pinna.

23. Massachusetts Fern

Dryopteris simulàta

Fronds:—Eight to twenty inches long, once *pinnate,* with partially divided *pinnæ,* the segments blunt and narrow. The fertile *fronds* are taller and more erect than the sterile and appear in midsummer.

Fruit-dots:—Medium sized, roundish and few in number. They are borne near the margins of the segments.

Rootstock:—Slender and creeping a little below the surface, sending up *fronds* at irregular intervals.

Habitat:—Deep shaded woods in moist situations.

Range:—The New England States, New York and Pennsylvania to Maryland and occasionally westward.

Distinguishing Mark:—Its general resemblance in aspect and color to the New York Fern, except that the lower *pinnæ* do *not* become gradually shorter until they practically disappear, but remain at about the same length as the middle *pinnæ.*

The novice will find the identification of this fern an interesting problem that will be most quickly solved by careful inspection of every colony of New York Ferns he encounters during woodland rambles. Stick to moist localities and look at the lower pinnæ, is the best procedure. Other vernacular names are Lance-leaved Marsh Fern and Bog Fern.

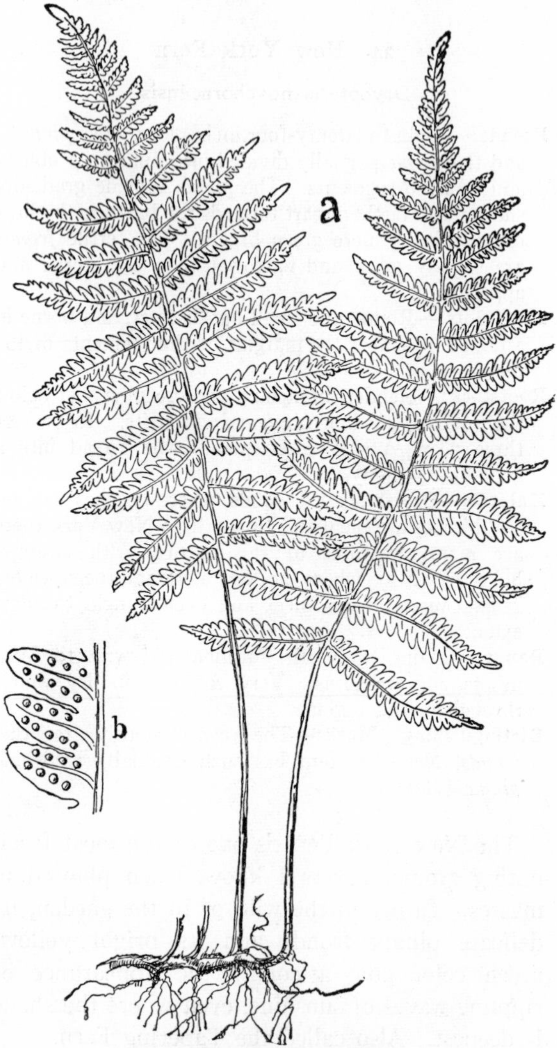

MASSACHUSETTS FERN

a. Ordinary Fronds; b. Section of Fruiting Pinna.

24. New York Fern

Dryopteris noveboracénsis

Fronds:—Eight to twenty-four inches long, once *pinnate,* and the *pinnæ* partially divided into numerous oblong and rounded segments. The *pinnæ* become gradually shorter and farther apart towards the bottom, the lowest pair being mere green bracts. The fertile *fronds* are slightly taller and narrower than the sterile and appear later.

Fruit-dots:—Round and small but distinct, and borne in a double row near the margins of the segments of the *pinnæ.*

Rootstock:—Slender, branching and creeping just below the surface, sending up *fronds* in tufts. In two or three years, a half dozen plants will spread into a good sized colony.

Habitat:—Dryish shaded woods, where beeches, maples and birches are plentiful. In southern New York there are many locations of this nature, with swampy hollows near by, where the New York and the so-called Massachusetts ferns meet and even mingle to some extent.

Range:—Maine to North Carolina and west to Minnesota and Arkansas. Very common in dry woods throughout this region.

Distinguishing Mark:—The conspicuously tapering *fronds.* No other fern has such gradually vanishing *pinnæ* below.

The New York Fern is one of the most fascinating ground covers I know, when planted in masses. Either in the wild or in the garden, its delicate plumy fronds and its bright yellow-green color give a colony the appearance of rippling waves of sunshine, even where the shade is deepest. Also called the Tapering Fern.

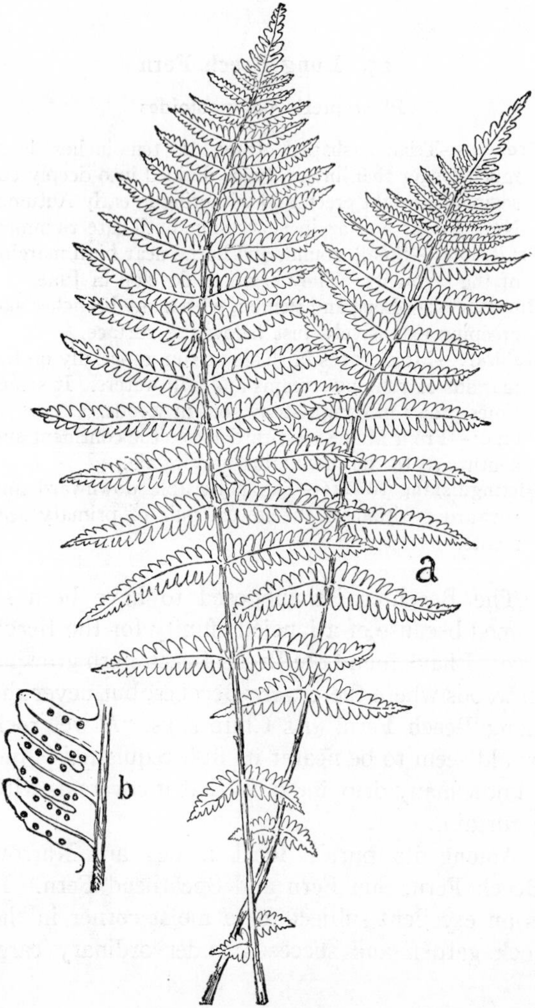

NEW YORK FERN

a. Ordinary Fronds; b. Section of Fruiting Pinna.

25. Long Beech Fern

Phegópteris polypodioides

Fronds:—Triangle-shaped, three to ten inches long, much longer than broad, twice divided into deeply cut segments, bright green and withering in early Autumn. New *fronds* appear in succession until late Summer.

Fruit-dots:—Small, round, and borne near both margins of the segments. They begin to develop in June.

Rootstocks:—Long and slender, with many branches and creeping extensively just below the surface.

Habitat:—Moist rocks in shade or sun, especially on the margins of running streams and still waters. It sometimes grows in damp, stony soil, in woods.

Range:—From Maine westward across the continent and southward to the mountains of Virginia.

Distinguishing Mark:—The noticeable downward and forward position of the lowest pair of primary segments.

The Beechfern is supposed to have been so named because of a fancied affinity for the Beech tree. I have found the Broad Beech Fern growing in woods where there were Beeches, but never the Long Beech Fern. As Clute says, "A wet rock would seem to be nearer its first requisite." And I know many dripping cliffs that it covers as with a curtain.

Among its purely local names are Narrow Beech Fern, Sun Fern and Spearhead Fern. It is an excellent subject for a moist corner in the rock garden and succeeds under ordinary care.

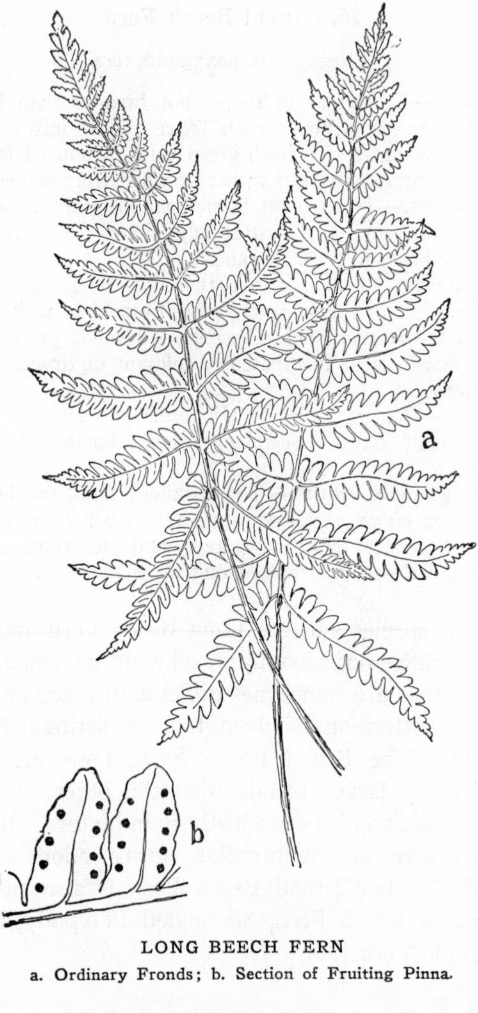

LONG BEECH FERN

a. Ordinary Fronds; b. Section of Fruiting Pinna.

26. Broad Beech Fern

Phegopteris hexagonóptera

Fronds:—Triangular in shape, but broader than long, (Five to ten inches broad). Twice divided into deeply cut segments, of a fresh green color, produced freely and continuously, but withering when frost comes.

Fruit-dots:—Tiny, round, borne near the margins of the segments and also scatteringly along the *midveins*. They begin to show in June.

Rootstocks:—Slenderer than those of the Long Beech Fern, but of the same creeping, branching habit.

Habitat:—Rather open to deep shaded woods, preferably in moist soil, but apparently tolerant of dryish situations.

Range:—Central Maine to Minnesota and southward to the Gulf states. Seemingly more abundant in the South.

Distinguishing Marks:—The strikingly large and broad bottom *pinnæ,* the lower segments of which are often much longer than the upper; and the continuous, irregularly shaped wings along the main stem.

This species and the Long Beech Fern appear to hybridize occasionally, producing intermediate forms that are sometimes difficult to place unless careful attention is given to the distinguishing marks. The Broad Beech Fern, however, has noticeably larger fronds than the other, stands more erect and is not so leathery in texture. Both kinds give out a peculiar, ferny odor when crushed. The Broad Beech Fern is also called Hexagon Beech Fern, Six-angled Polypody, and Triangle Fern.

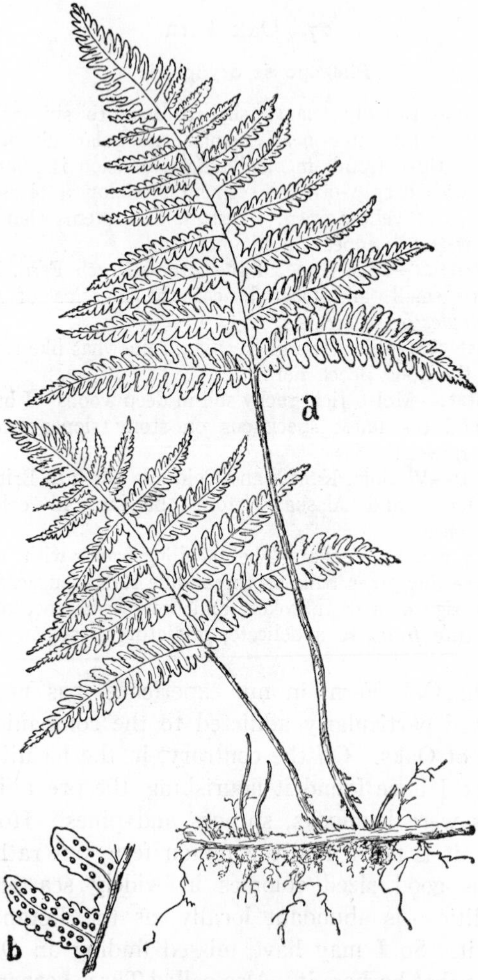

BROAD BEECH FERN

a. Ordinary Fronds; b. Section of Fruiting Pinna.

27. Oak Fern

Phegopteris dryópteris

Fronds:—Broadly triangle-shaped, four to six inches wide, with three nearly equal triangular divisions, "like three fronds in one." Each division is *pinnate* or with deeply divided segments. Color, a pleasing shade of yellow-green. Texture thin, stems slender. New *fronds* appear all summer long.

Fruit-dots:—Like those of the Broad Beech Fern, but very small, and located near the margins of the *pinnules* or segments.

Rootstocks:—Slender and creeping, somewhat like those of the Long Beech Fern.

Habitat:—Moist, rich, rocky soil in deep woods. I have found the finest specimens on stony slopes under evergreens.

Range:—Virginia, Kansas and Colorado north to British America and Alaska. More abundant in colder regions.

Distinguishing Marks:—The uncoiling *fronds* with their three tiny green balls on thread-like stalks, suggesting the sign of a pawnbroker; and the resemblance of a mature *frond* to a delicate, miniature Bracken.

The Oak Fern, in my experience, has never seemed particularly addicted to the companionship of Oaks. On the contrary, in the localities where I have found it flourishing, the prevailing trees were hemlocks, spruces and pines. However, it is not a really common fern, but rather forms good sized colonies in widely scattered localities—is abundant locally, as the Botanies put it. So I may have missed finding an Oak grove that harbors it. Also called Three-cornered Fern.

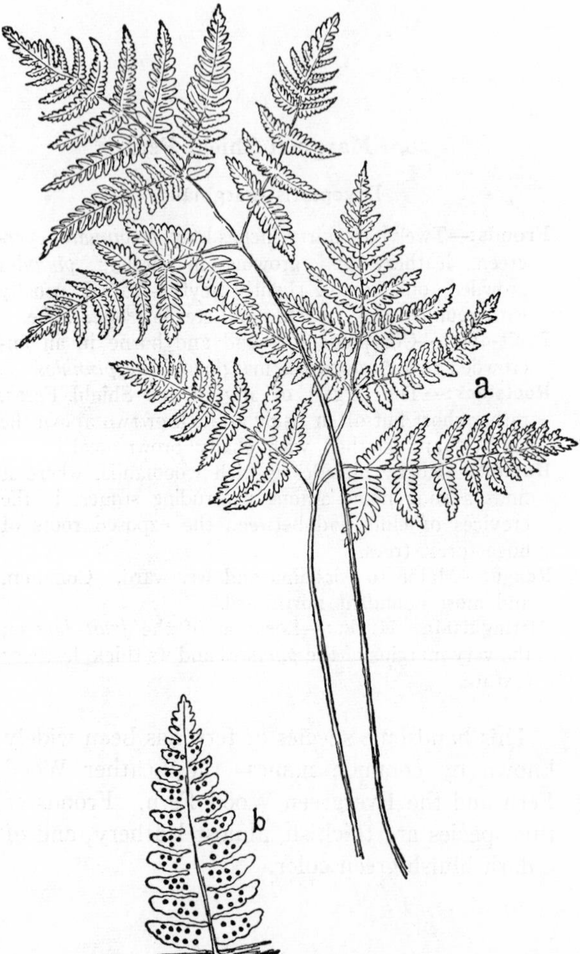

OAK FERN

a. Ordinary Fronds; b. Fruiting Pinnule.

28. Marginal Shield Fern

Dryopteris marginàlis

Fronds:—Twelve to thirty inches long, *bi-pinnate,* evergreen, leathery and growing in circles: *pinnules* crowded, oblong and slightly scythe-shaped, usually with rounded tips. Fertile and sterile *fronds* alike.

Fruit-dots:—Conspicuous, round and borne in an uncrowded row close to the margins of the *pinnules.*

Rootstock:—The largest of any of the Shield Ferns, rather short but often rising an inch or two above the surface, and clothed with chaffy brown scales.

Habitat:—Rocky hillsides in rich woodlands, where it finds a snug home among protruding stones, in the crevices of cliffs and between the exposed roots of huge forest trees.

Range:—Maine to Alabama and westward. Common, and most abundant northward.

Distinguishing Marks:—Location of the *fruit-dots* on the very margins of the *pinnules* and its thick, leathery texture.

This handsome species of fern has been widely known by common names—the Leather Wood Fern and the Evergreen Wood Fern. Fronds of this species are thickish, almost leathery, and of a dark bluish-green color.

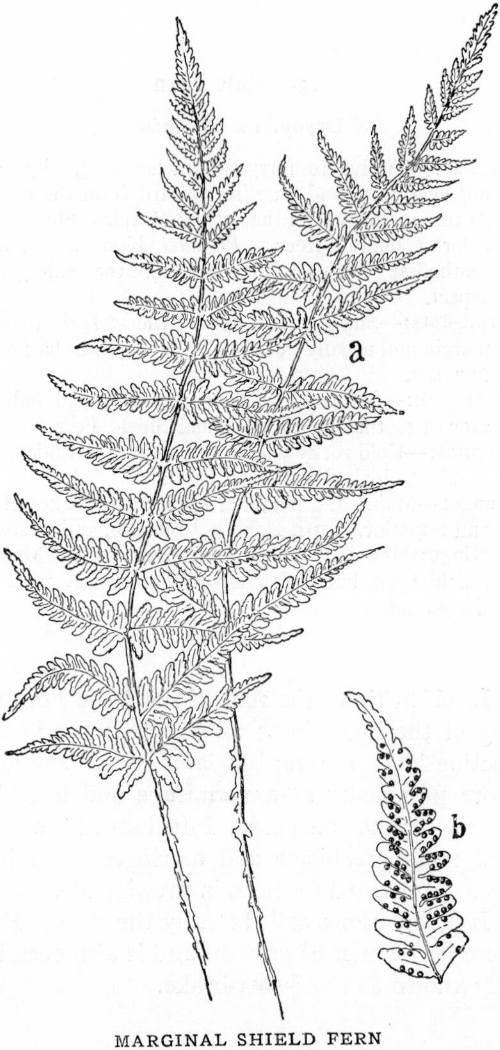

MARGINAL SHIELD FERN

a. Ordinary Fronds; b. Fruiting Pinna.

29. Male Fern

Dryopteris fìlix-más

Fronds:—Twelve to forty-two inches long, *bi-pinnate, not* evergreen, and tapering upward from the bottom. Texture thinner than that of the Marginal Shield Fern, color a lighter green. *Pinnules* blunt and sharply toothed at the tips. Otherwise have the same general aspect.

Fruit-dots:—Small, round, nearer the *midvein* than the margin and usually borne only on the lower half of the *pinnules.*

Rootstock:—Similar in size, appearance and habit of growth to that of the Marginal Shield Fern.

Habitat:—Cold rocky woods, in northern latitudes, or at middle to high elevations southward.

Range:—Maine and northern Vermont to Lakes Huron and Superior, North Dakota, Colorado, and westward.

Distinguishing Marks:—Resemblance to the Marginal Shield Fern, but with *fruit-dots* differently placed on the *pinnules.*

In olden times the root of the Male Fern was one of the ingredients used by witches in concocting love-philters; but later it was employed more practically as a vermifuge and is still in repute for that purpose. Infusions of the stems and roots are bitter and astringent and have been substituted for hops in brewing ale.

It is sometimes called locally the Basket Fern, from its manner of growth, and is also occasionally known as the Sweet-brake.

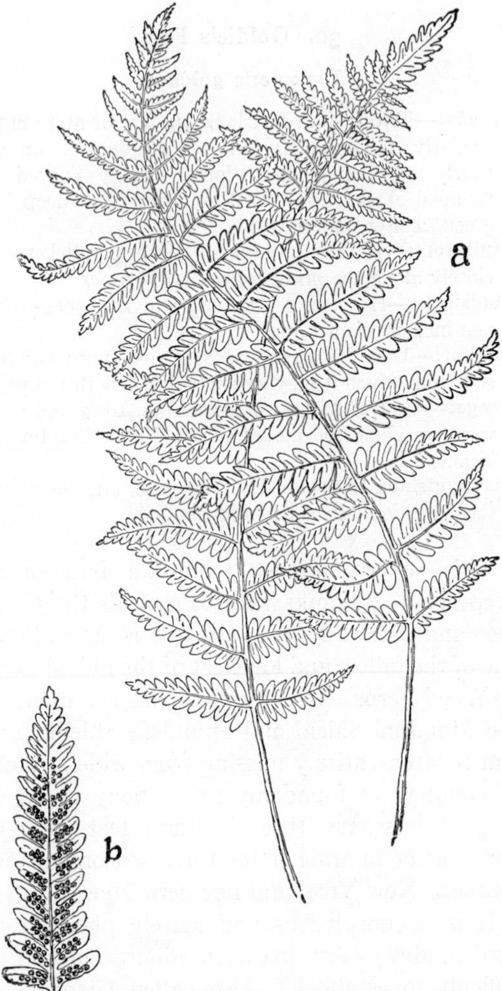

MALE FERN

a. Ordinary Fronds; b. Fruiting Pinna.

30. Goldie's Fern

Dryopteris goldiàna

Fronds:—Two to four feet long, six feet or more in particularly favorable localities. *Bi-pinnate,* or very nearly so, the *pinnules* long, slightly curved and rounded at the tips. Texture firm, color deep blue-green, lighter underneath.

Fruit-dots:—Rather large and borne parallel to and closely along the *midveins* of the *pinnules.*

Rootstock:—Horizontal, creeping and from one-half to one inch in diameter.

Habitat:—Deep but open woods, in rich, moist and loose soil from which it may easily be lifted with the hands.

Range:—Central Maine to Minnesota, Iowa and southward, reaching the mountains of North Carolina and Tennessee.

Distinguishing Marks:—Its great size, and location of the *fruit-dots* along the midveins.

This superb, almost Palm-like fern of the deepest woods, ranks with or exceeds the Cinnamon and Ostrich ferns in size. It is far and away one of the tallest and loveliest of the Shield Ferns, or Wood Ferns. It is by no means common, like the Marginal Shield and Spinulose Shield Ferns, and is often entirely missing from wide stretches of country. I found my first colony in an unsuspected swamp, three hundred feet from my home, after hunting it for three seasons all over southern New York and northern New Jersey.

It is a conspicuous and stately plant in the garden, always exciting keen admiration and not difficult to establish. Also called Giant Wood Fern.

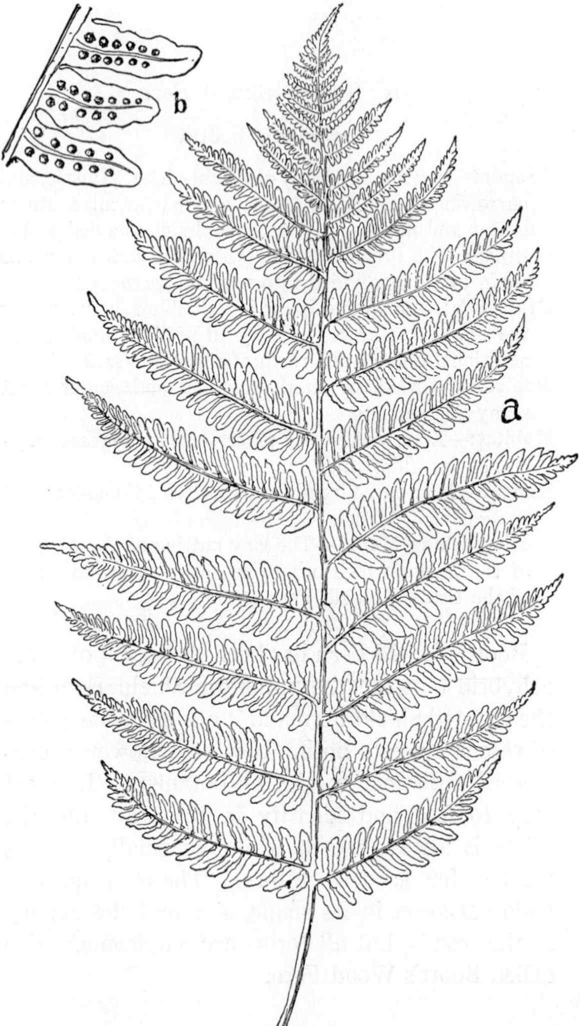

GOLDIE'S FERN

a. Ordinary Frond; b. Section of Fruiting Pinna.

31. Boott's Shield Fern

Dryopteris boóttii

Fronds:—Fifteen to twenty-six inches long, *pinnate,* and narrowing at the base: lowest *pinnæ* triangular, others longer and narrower: *pinnules* oblong, rounded at the tip and with bristled teeth. Those of the lower *pinnæ* again partially divided into toothed segments.

Fruit-dots:—Small and borne in a double row quite near the *midvein,* with a tendency to produce one or two additional dots on the teeth of the *pinnules.*

Rootstock:—Medium sized, creeping and sending out many fine rootlets.

Habitat:—Low, wet, shady places, with a marked preference for alder thickets.

Range:—Maine to Virginia and west to Minnesota: Reported from Alaska.

Distinguishing Mark:—The lacy cutting of the *pinnules* of the *fronds* which otherwise closely resemble those of the Crested Shield Fern.

Boott's Shield Fern has been suspected of being a hybrid between the Spinulose Shield Fern and the Crested Shield Fern and it certainly has points of resemblance to both. It is now, however, considered a distinct species by botanists. It is not easy to find and identify in the wild, but the effort is always worth while, especially if it is wanted for garden culture. There is quite a wide variation in its shape, size and the cutting of the fronds, but all forms are handsome. Also called Boott's Wood Fern.

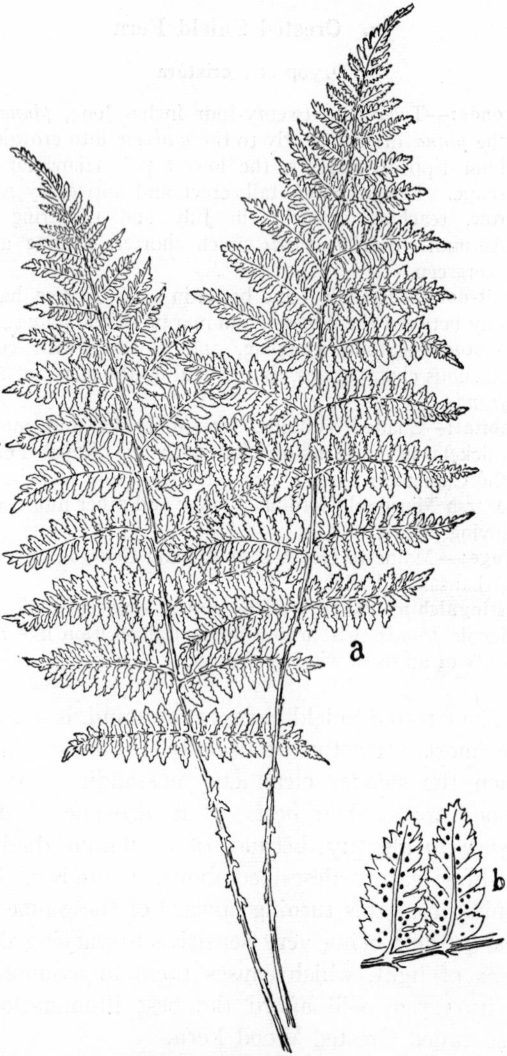

BOOTT'S SHIELD FERN

a. Ordinary Fronds; b. Fruiting Pinnules.

32. Crested Shield Fern

Dryopteris cristàta

Fronds:—Twelve to twenty-four inches long, *pinnate,* the *pinnæ* divided nearly to the *midvein* into crowded, blunt-tipped segments, the lowest pair triangular in shape. Fertile *fronds* tall, erect and noticeably narrow, reaching maturity in July and withering in Autumn. Sterile *fronds* much shorter, arching and evergreen.

Fruit-dots:—Roundish and borne in a double row, halfway between the *midvein* and margin of the *pinnæ.*

Rootstock:—Stout, creeping, and covered with conspicuous chaffy scales, that extend up the stems of the *fronds.*

Habitat:—Shaded swamps, stream banks and moist thickets in close association with the Royal Fern, the Cinnamon Fern, Skunk Cabbage, False Hellebore, Marsh Marigold, Cardinal Flower and other moisture-loving plants.

Range:—Maine to North Carolina and Georgia, west to Arkansas and Idaho.

Distinguishing Marks:—The *pinnæ,* especially of the fertile *fronds* twist into a horizontal position like the slats of an open window shutter.

The Crested Shield Fern, to my mind, is one of the most attractive, especially in midsummer when the slender clean cut, upstanding fertile fronds are at their best. It is also one of the easiest to identify, because of its unique distinguishing feature, described above. Clute is of the opinion that this turning upward of the pinnæ is due to their being very sensitive to varying degrees of light, which causes them to assume a position that will afford the best illumination. Also called Crested Wood Fern.

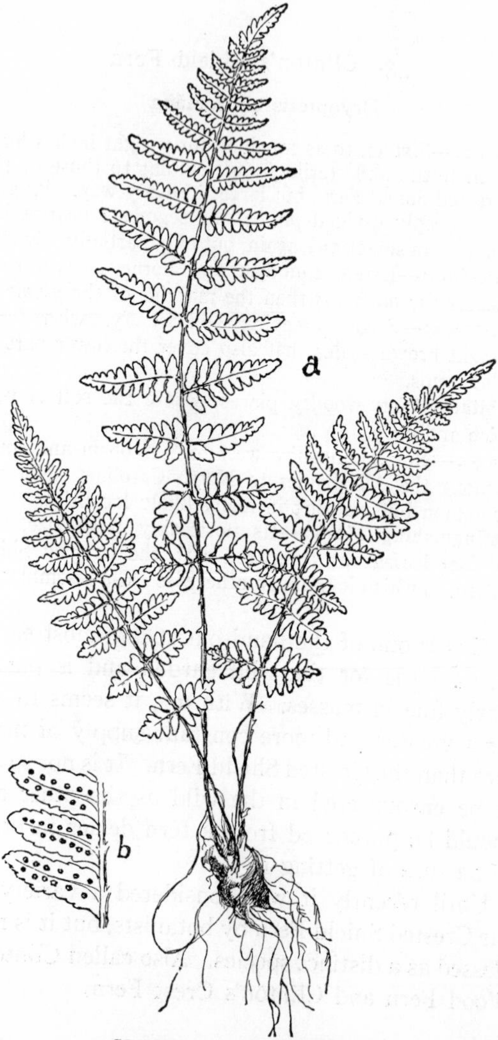

CRESTED SHIELD FERN

a. Ordinary Fronds; b. Section of Fruiting Pinna.

33. Clinton's Shield Fern

Dryopteris clintoniàna

Fronds:—Sixteen to as much as forty-eight inches long, both fertile and sterile *fronds* similar to those of the Crested Shield Fern, but larger in every way. *Pinnate* with deeply divided *pinnæ,* the segments nearest the main stem sometimes again, but only partially, divided.

Fruit-dots:—Large, roundish and borne in two rows nearer the *midveins* than the margins of the *pinnæ.*

Rootstock:—Stout, creeping and chaffy, with large bright brown scales that also cover the lower part of the stems.

Habitat:—Wet, woodsy places, where the soil is very rich and deep.

Range:—New Hampshire west to Wisconsin and south among the Alleghanies to North Carolina. Not uncommon but wanting in many likely localities.

Distinguishing Mark:—Its noticeably large size, and denser leafage as compared with the Crested Shield Fern, to which it bears an otherwise close resemblance.

This is one of the handsomest and most easily grown ferns for the wild garden and is particularly fine in masses. With me, it seems to ask for a greater and more constant supply of moisture than the Crested Shield Fern. It is not so apt to be encountered in the wild as the other and should be purchased from a fern dealer in order to be sure of getting it.

Until recently it was considered a variety of the Crested Shield Fern by botanists, but it is now classed as a distinct species. Also called Clinton's Wood Fern and Clinton's Crest Fern.

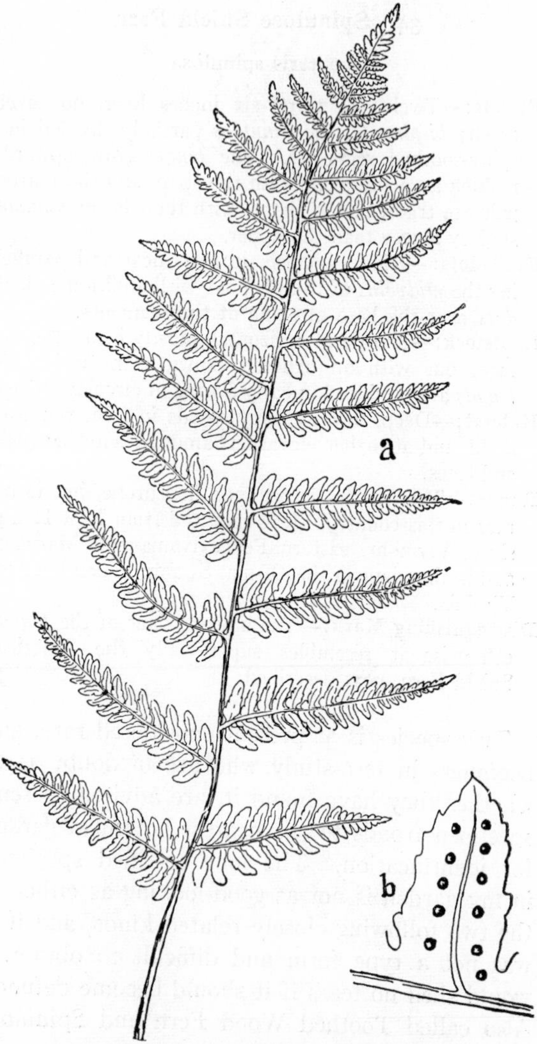

CLINTON'S SHIELD FERN
a. Ordinary Frond; b. Fruiting Pinnules.

34. Spinulose Shield Fern

Dryopteris spinulòsa

Fronds:—Twelve to thirty-six inches long, not evergreen; *bi-pinnate*, the *pinnules* partially divided into spiny-toothed segments. The *pinnæ* grow upwards, making an acute angle with the stem, and the bottom pair are triangular in shape, with their lower *pinnules* slightly longer than the upper.

Fruit-dots:—Kidney-shaped, in rows near and paralleling the *midveins* of the *pinnules* with additional single *dots* near the base of some of the segments.

Rootstock:—Short and horizontal, mostly below the surface, but with an exposed crown from which the *fronds* are produced in early Spring in circular clumps.

Habitat:—Deep, low, swampy woods in rich, wet leaf-mold, and at higher elevations among sheltering rocks and trees.

Range:—This species is common in Europe, but rather rare in this country. It is reported from New Hampshire, Vermont, eastern Pennsylvania and Maryland and is abundant in the Dismal Swamp in southeastern Virginia.

Distinguishing Mark:—The upward slant of the *pinnæ;* otherwise it resembles superficially the American Shield Fern, next described.

This species is at present considered rare, and beginners in fern-study who are in doubt as to whether they have found it, are advised to send specimen fronds to the nearest botanical garden for identification. The lone certified specimen in my garden is not as good-looking as either of the two following closely related kinds, and if it was not a type form and difficult to obtain, I would shed no tears if it should become defunct. Also called Toothed Wood Fern and Spinulose Wood Fern.

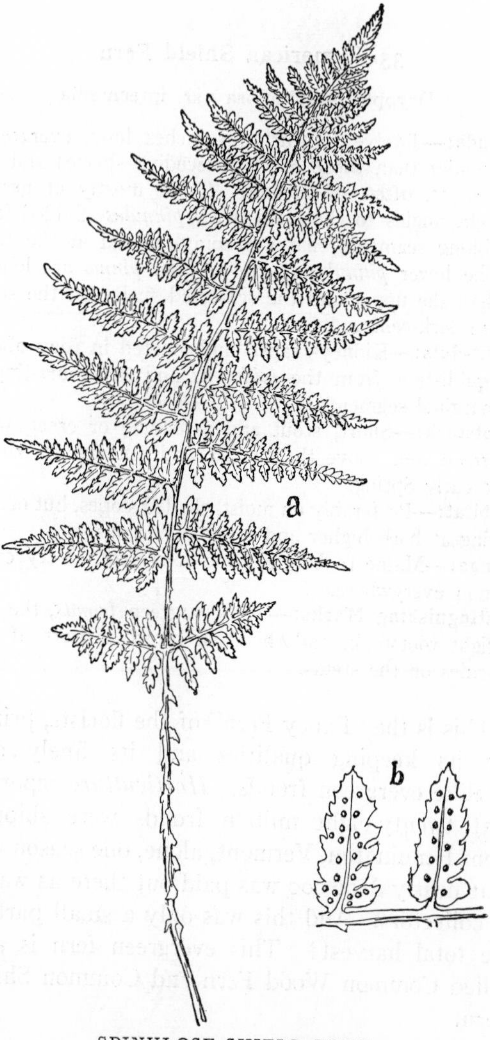

SPINULOSE SHIELD FERN

a. Ordinary Frond; b. Fruiting Pinnules.

35. American Shield Fern

Dryopteris spinulosa var. intermèdia

Fronds:—Twelve to thirty-six inches long, evergreen, broader than those of the preceding species and *bi-pinnate,* often *tri-pinnate. Pinnæ* mostly at nearly right angles to the stem, with *pinnules* divided into oblong segments that are spiny-toothed at the tips. The lower *pinnules* of the bottom *pinnæ* are longer than the upper and the scattered scales on the stem are dark-centered.

Fruit-dots:—Kidney-shaped and located in rows about equidistant from the *midveins* and the spiny-tipped marginal segments.

Rootstock:—Short, stout and ascending or erect, with crown well above the surface and sending up *fronds* in early Spring.

Habitat:—Preferably on moist, shaded slopes, but occurring at both higher and lower elevations.

Range:—Maine to Virginia and westward. Very common everywhere.

Distinguishing Marks:—The evergreen *fronds,* the upright rootstock, and the dark brown centers of the scales on the stems.

This is the "Fancy Fern" of the florists, prized for its keeping qualities and its finely cut, lacelike evergreen fronds. *Horticulture* reported that twenty-eight million fronds were shipped from Bennington, Vermont, alone, one season and that nearly $100,000 was paid out there as wages to collectors. And this was only a small part of the total harvest! This evergreen fern is also called Common Wood Fern and Common Shield Fern.

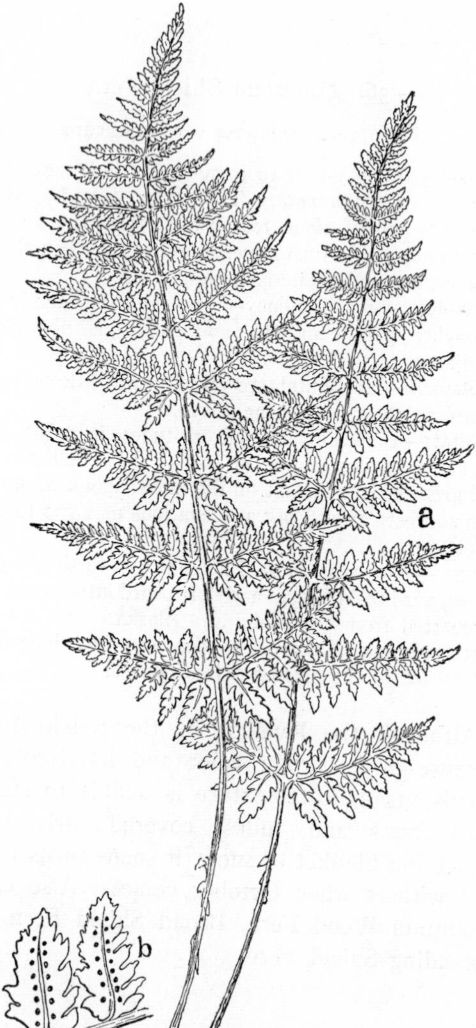

AMERICAN SHIELD FERN
a. Ordinary Fronds; b. Fruiting Pinnules.

36. Mountain Shield Fern

Dryopteris spinulosa var. americàna

Fronds:—Twenty-four to forty inches long, not always evergreen, *bi-pinnate*. The lower *pinnules* of the bottom pair of *pinnæ* from two to three times as long as the upper. Much larger in every way than the two preceding and related species.

Fruit-dots:—Small, kidney-shaped, and arranged in rows roughly paralleling the *midveins*, but not closely adjacent.

Rootstock.—Horizontal, creeping at or a little below the surface, the crown rising above.

Habitat:—Preferably at high altitudes, in moist somewhat acid leaf-mold, on rock and boulder-strewn slopes. It is abundant on the Shawangunk Mountains in southern New York at elevations of 1,200 to 2,200 feet.

Range:—Northern New England to North Carolina, westward to Michigan and northward into Canada. Is reported from Greenland and Alaska.

Distinguishing Mark:—The conspicuously long lower *pinnules* of the bottom pair of *pinnæ*.

Although the loveliest of the Shield Ferns, because of its bright color and its deeply cut fronds, its delicate texture is unable to survive hard frosts and, unless covered early by a protecting blanket of snow, it soons turns brown and withers when October comes. Also called Mountain Wood Fern, Broad Shield Fern, and Spreading Shield Fern.

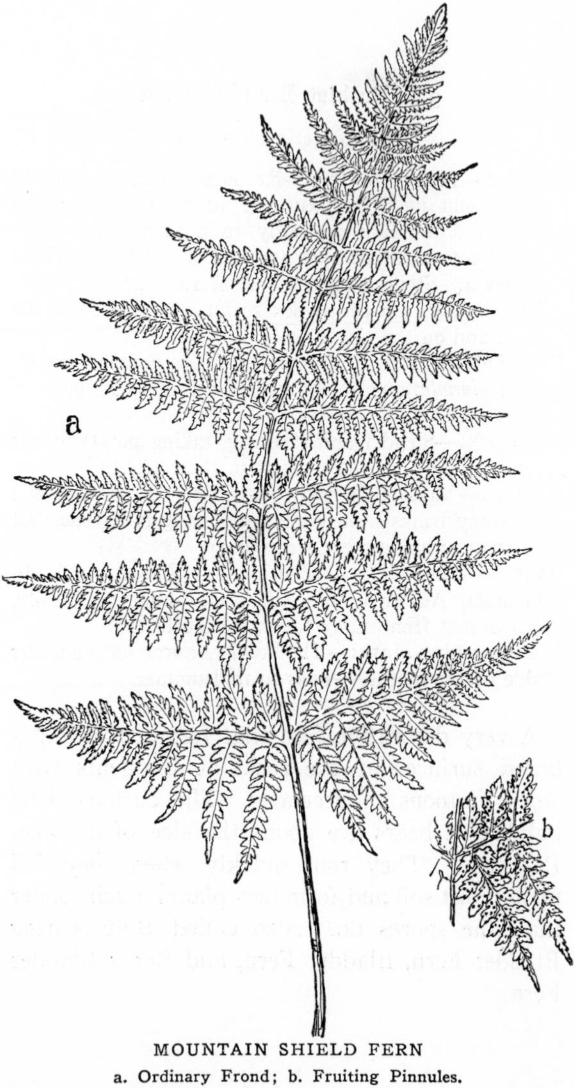

MOUNTAIN SHIELD FERN

a. Ordinary Frond; b. Fruiting Pinnules.

37. Bulblet Bladder Fern

Cystópteris bulbífera

Fronds:—Twelve to thirty-six inches long, frequently forty-eight inches; mature in July. Widest at the base and tapering gradually to a long slender tip. *Bi-pinnate* with crowded, toothed or partially divided *pinnules.* Stems wingless. Most fully grown *fronds* bear bulblets on the under surface, usually near the stem and on the upper half.

Fruit-dots:—Small and roundish in a double row on each *pinnule,* one dot near the base of each tooth or *segment.*

Rootstock:—Slender and creeping, taking possession of close-by crevices and pockets in the rocks.

Habitat:—Moist cliffs and rocks in shaded ravines and on stony banks near water, preferring limestone, but tolerant of moderately acid soil.

Range:—Maine to Wisconsin and Iowa, south to Georgia, Alabama and Arkansas; abundant locally, but absent from many favorable localities.

Distinguishing Mark:—The bulblets borne on the under side of the mature *fronds* in midsummer.

A very decorative fern that frequently drapes broad surfaces of the rocks it frequents with dense festoons of greenery. The curious little bulblets it bears are about the size of a Sweet Pea seed. They root quickly when they fall upon moist soil and form new plants much sooner than the spores do. Also called Bulb-bearing Bladder Fern, Bladder Fern, and Berry Bladder Fern.

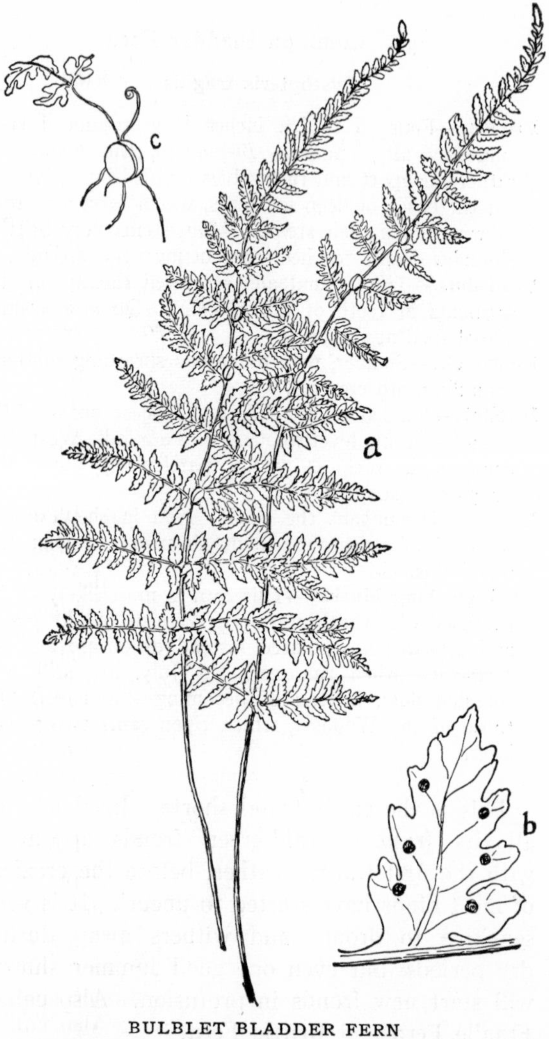

BULBLET BLADDER FERN

a. Ordinary Fronds; b. Fruiting Pinnule; c. Young Fern growing from Bulblet.

38. Common Bladder Fern

Cystópteris frágilis

Fronds:—Four to twelve inches long, produced continuously all Summer. *Bi-pinnate,* the *pinnæ* set rather far apart and themselves divided into *pinnules* (at the base) or deep segments, which form a margin or wing along their stems. Main stems very brittle. *Pinnules* deeply toothed, the cutting very variable.

Fruit-dots.—Tiny, round and scattered thickly on the segments or teeth of the *pinnules.* Do *not* become star-shaped at maturity.

Rootstock:—Slender, with numerous spreading rootlets, extending into crevices.

Habitat:—Shaded rocks, cliffs and ledges; occasionally in moist, stony, level woods. In the middle West it is common in rockless woods, particularly along the margins of streams.

Range:—Throughout the world, even in the Tropics, where it flourishes at high elevations among the mountains.

Distinguishing Marks:—This fern is most likely to be confused with the Blunt-lobed Woodsia but its *pinnæ* and *pinnules* are pointed instead of obtuse and its *fruit-dots,* when ripe early in July, are still wee rounded dots, instead of becoming star-shaped like those of the Woodsia, which ripen some two weeks later.

This is the earliest and shortest lived fern of all, its fresh emerald-green fronds appearing with the first warm weather, before the croziers of most kinds have started to uncurl. It is very sensitive to drouth and withers away during dry periods, but even one good summer shower will start new fronds in profusion. Also called Fragile Fern and Brittle Fern.

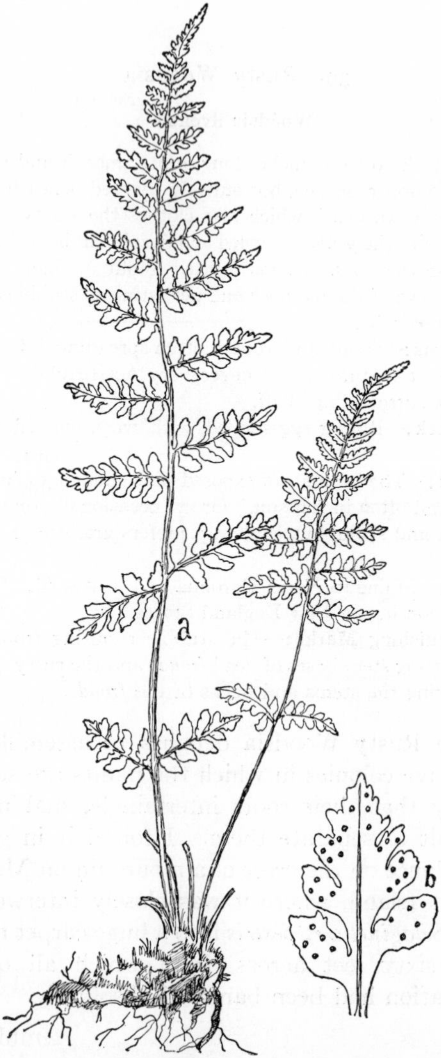

COMMON BLADDER FERN
a. Ordinary Fronds; b. Fruiting Pinnule

39. Rusty Woodsia

Woódsia ilvénsis

Fronds:—Two to six inches long, quite smooth and green on the upper surface, but entirely covered beneath with rusty-brown chaff, which also clothes the stems. *Pinnate*, with the *pinnæ* crowded and deeply cut into oblong, obtuse segments. Stems jointed about an inch above the crown of the *rootstock* and persisting as stubble after the *fronds* die.

Fruit-dots:—Small and round, often spreading into each other at maturity, but never very noticeable because of the surrounding chaff.

Rootstock:—Rather egg-shaped, with wiry, matted rootlets.

Habitat:—The summits of exposed cliffs and ledges, in acid soil and often in full sun. Grows occasionally on sandstone and shale, but evidently prefers granitic or trap-rocks.

Range:—Maine to North Carolina and westward. Quite common in the New England States.

Distinguishing Marks:—The stubble resulting from the persisting stem-bases of dead *fronds* and the rusty scales covering the stems and backs of the *fronds*.

The Rusty Woodsia delights to assemble in extensive colonies in which the plants are set so closely that their roots intermingle, making it difficult to separate them. I found it in great abundance on the crest of a mountain on Mount Desert Island, where it was closely interwoven with *Selaginella rupestris* into a huge carpet more than sixty feet across, from which all other vegetation had been banished absolutely.

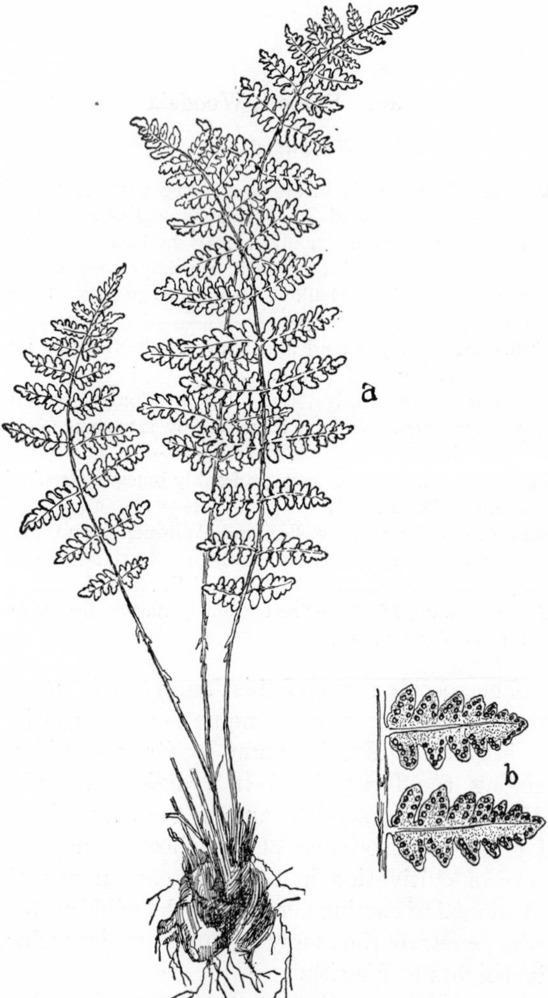

RUSTY WOODSIA

a. Ordinary Fronds; b. Fruiting Pinnules.

40. Smooth Woodsia

Woódsia glabélla

Fronds:—Two to six inches long, very narrow, smooth on both sides and of extremely delicate texture. *Pinnate*, the *pinnæ* far apart near the base, somewhat crowded near the tip; roundish, egg-shaped and slightly parted into three shallow, rounded segments. Stems straw-colored.

Fruit-dots:—Tiny, round and scanty, only three or four on the back of each *pinna*.

Rootstock:—Diminutive, but often with long thread-like rootlets where they have room to grow into some pocket or crevice.

Habitat:—On moist, mossy, preferably limestone rocks in slightly alkaline soil.

Range:—Northern New England, Adirondack and Catskill mountains, New York, to the far North and Northwest. Reported from Alaska and Greenland.

Distinguishing Mark:—The extremely narrow fronds and straw-colored stems.

The specific name of this fern, *glabella*, means smooth, so its common name is a translation. It is given no English name by Gray and is not among the ferns listed in *Standardized Plant Names.* It is included among the fifty selected for this book, because of its delicate beauty, its ease of cultivation in the rock garden and the likelihood of coming across it in the wild by those who penetrate the mossy mountain ravines where it delights to flourish.

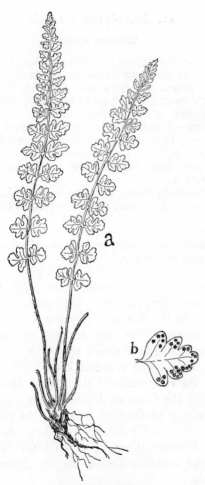

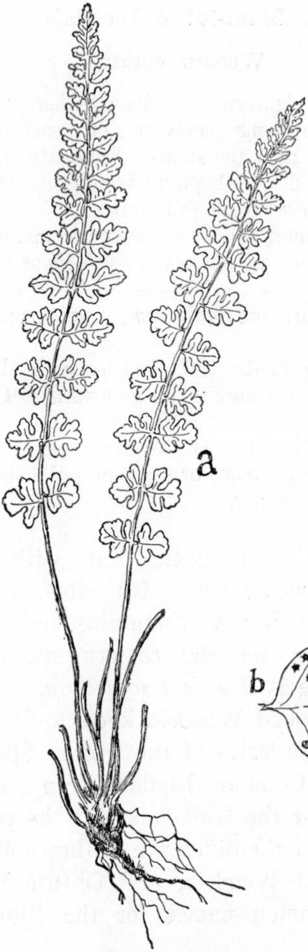

SMOOTH WOODSIA

a. Ordinary Fronds; b. Fruiting Pinna.

41. Blunt-lobed Woodsia

Woódsia obtùsa

Fronds:—Six to eighteen inches long, *pinnate,* the widely spaced, obtuse *pinnæ* deeply cut, or sometimes themselves *pinnate* near the stems. Segments oblong and slightly toothed. Both *pinnules* and segments blunt at the tips. Evergreen southward.

Fruit-dots:—Round and borne near the margin of the segments, becoming noticeably star-shaped in early Summer.

Rootstock:—Short and horizontal, sending out numerous rootlets.

Habitat:—Rocky banks, cliffs, and ledges in shade.

Range:—Maine to Georgia and westward to Oklahoma and Arizona.

Distinguishing Marks:—The blunted tips of both the *pinnæ* and the *pinnules,* or segments; the star-shaped *fruit-dots* in Summer.

A closely similar species, but with shorter fronds and inconspicuous fruit-dots, is rather common in the Rocky Mountains and is sometimes mistaken for the eastern species. Its botanical name is *Woodsia scopulina.*

The Blunt-lobed Woodsia keeps quite closely within the boundaries of the United States. It resembles the Common Bladder Fern somewhat, but a glance at the fruit-dots and the pinnæ of either will show the difference. Blunt-lobed Cliff Fern, Common Woodsia, and Obtuse Woodsia are other common names for the Blunt-lobed Woodsia.

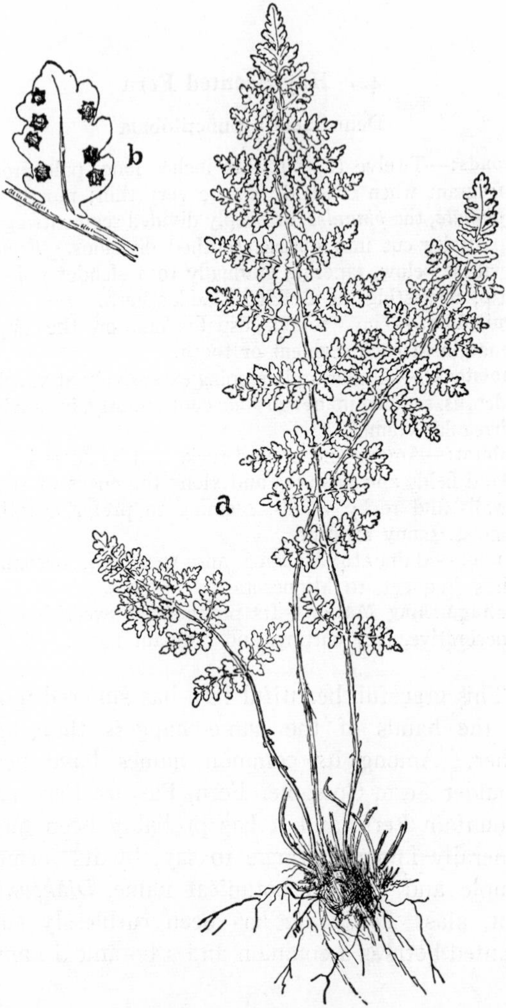

BLUNT-LOBED WOODSIA

a. Ordinary Fronds; b. Fruiting Pinnule.

42. Hay-Scented Fern

Dennstaédtia punctilóbula

Fronds:—Twelve to thirty-six inches long, pale green, fragrant when crushed, texture very thin; mostly *bi-pinnate,* the *pinnules,* or deeply divided segments again partially cut into obtuse, toothed divisions. *Fronds* widest below, tapering gradually to a slender pointed tip, suggesting the Bulblet Bladder Fern.

Fruit-dots:—Tiny, round, usually one on the upper margin of each segment or tooth.

Rootstock:—Slender and creeping extensively at varying depths, sending up new *fronds* continuously, in tangled, irregular clumps.

Habitat:—Among and around rocks and boulders in upland fields and pastures and along the edges of stone walls and rocky woods, seeming to prefer a rather moist, sunny exposure.

Range:—Maine to Alabama and westward, becoming less frequent, to Minnesota.

Distinguishing Marks:—Its pronounced sweetish odor, decorative, lacy cutting, and rampant habit.

This graceful, beautiful fern has suffered more at the hands of the name-changers than any other. Among its common names have been Boulder Fern, Gossamer Fern, Pasture Fern and Mountain Fern, and it has probably been most generally known, strange to say, by its former, simple and musical botanical name *Dicksonia.* But, alas! *Dicksonia* has been ruthlessly supplanted both as a common and a botanical name

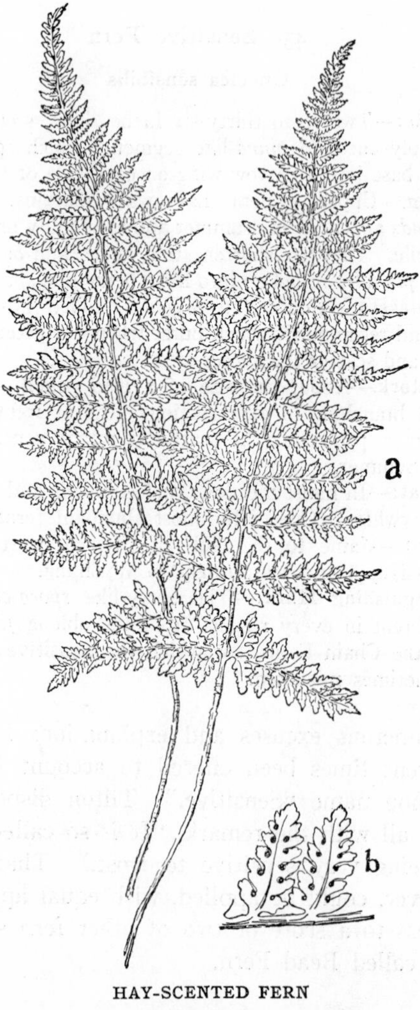

HAY-SCENTED FERN
a. Ordinary Fronds; b. Fruiting Pinnules.

43. Sensitive Fern

Onoclèa sensíbilis

Fronds:—Twelve to thirty-six inches long, sterile ones deeply cut into *pinna*-like segments which spread at the base into a narrow wing on each side of the main stem. Upper segments have wavy margins. Fertile *fronds* appear in midsummer and are totally unlike the sterile. They are shorter, stiffly erect, and *bi-pinnate*, the *pinnules* rolled up into little berry-like *spore-cases*.

Spore-cases:—Contracted *pinnules*, rolled into small, round receptacles, which burst when dry after maturity and scatter the *spores*.

Rootstock.—About the size of a lead pencil, creeping and branching in all directions near or right at the surface, producing the scattered *fronds* continuously all Summer.

Habitat:—In moist meadows, fields, woods and thickets everywhere. One of the most abundant ferns.

Range:—Maine to the Gulf of Mexico, west to the Mississippi and scatteringly to Wyoming.

Distinguishing Mark:—The berry-like *spore-cases*, so different in every respect from the oblong *fruit-dots* of the Chain Ferns, for which the Sensitive Fern is sometimes mistaken.

Numerous excuses and explanations have at different times been offered to account for the common name "Sensitive." Tilton disposes of them all with the remark, "It is so called from its being very sensitive to frost." That trait, however, could be applied, with equal appropriateness to a score or two of other fern species. Also called Bead Fern.

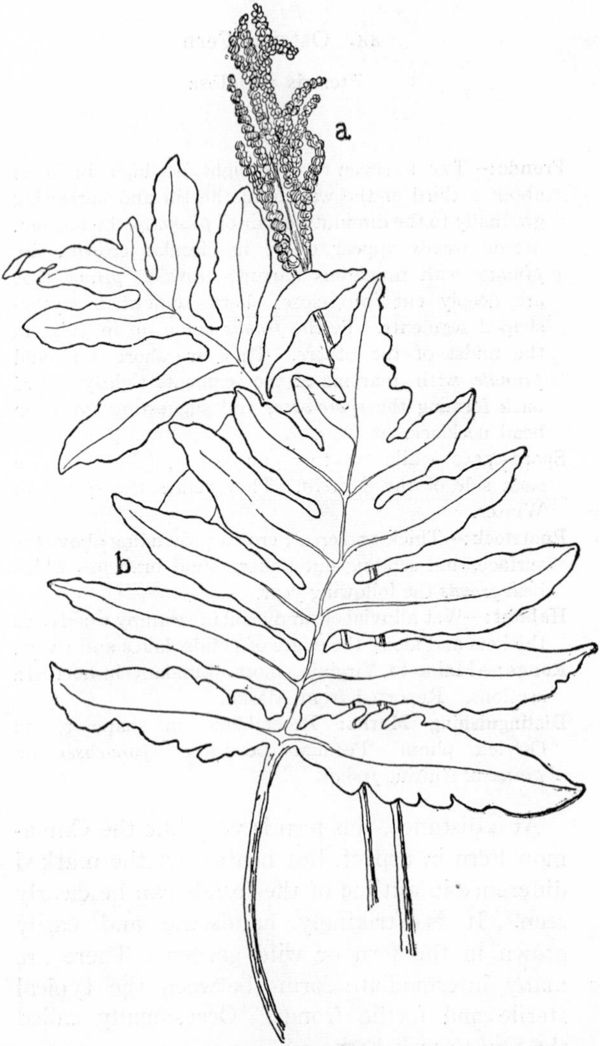

SENSITIVE FERN

a. Fertile Frond; b. Sterile Frond.

44. Ostrich Fern

Pteretis nodulòsa

Fronds:—Two to seven or even eight feet high, broadest about a third of the way from the tip and narrowing gradually to the diminutive pair of *pinnæ* at the bottom. Sterile *fronds* appear early, in circular crowns, are *pinnate* with numerous narrow, crowded *pinnæ* that are deeply cut into close, short, somewhat scythe-shaped segments. Fertile *fronds* come up in July, in the midst of the others. They are short, stiff and *pinnate* with margins of the segments tightly rolled back forming the *spore-cases* and suggesting an open bead necklace.

Spore-cases:—Like two tiny gun-barrels, (Clute) one on each side of the *midvein*. They retain the *spores* all Winter.

Rootstock:—Thick and erect, crown protruding above the surface, and sending out underground branches which bear *fronds* the following year.

Habitat:—Wet alluvial or sandy soil in swampy woods and thickets and along the edges of ponds, lakes and rivers.

Range:—Maine to Virginia, most abundant in northern sections. Reported from Alaska.

Distinguishing Marks:—Resemblance in shape to an Ostrich plume. Peculiar bead-like *spore-cases* on *pinnæ* of fruiting *fronds*.

At a distance, this fern is very like the Cinnamon Fern in aspect, but nearer by, the marked difference in outline of the fronds can be clearly seen. It is strikingly handsome and easily grown in the fern or wild garden. There are many intermediate forms between the typical sterile and fertile fronds. Occasionally called the Shuttlecock Fern.

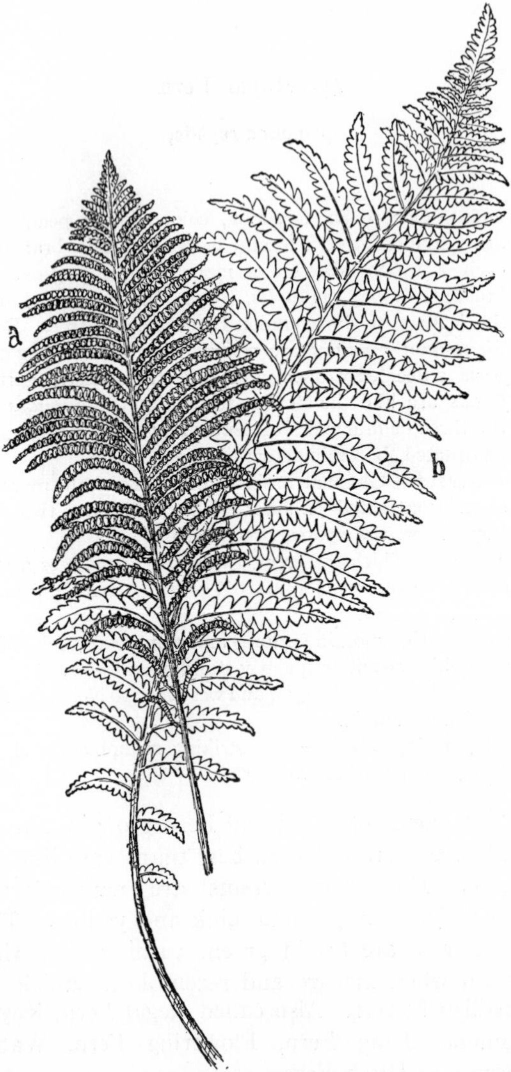

OSTRICH FERN

a. Fertile Frond; b. Sterile Frond.

45. Royal Fern

Osmúnda regàlis,

Fronds:—One to six feet long, color Nile or pea-green. Stem divides into five to nine pairs of opposite branches, each of which bears six or more pairs of long-oval or broadly oblong *pinnules*, resembling quite closely the leaflets of the common Black Locust tree. Both *pinnæ* and *pinnules* are widely separated, giving the *frond* a decidedly open and graceful aspect. Fertile *fronds* are like the sterile except that the *pinnules* of the three or four pairs of *pinnæ* at the top are greatly contracted, becoming stem-like.

Spore-cases:—Globular in shape and borne on the margins of the contracted *pinnules*. They split into two sections when the spores become ripe.

Rootstock:—Thick and erect, the crown sometimes a foot above the surface, the matted rootlets forming a large circular mound.

Habitat:—Common in swamps and wet woods, delighting in liquid ooze and frequently standing in water.

Range:—Maine to Georgia, and westward to Nebraska and British Columbia.

Distinguishing Mark:—The striking resemblance of its foliage to that of the Locust.

The fronds of the Royal Fern grow in clumps that are pyramidal rather than vase-like in shape. The young stems are wine-colored, and the uncoiling pinnæ pink and yellow. The spore-cases are bright green, turning to a rich brown when mature and resemble a panicle of smallish flowers. Also called Regal Fern, Royal Osmund, King Fern, Flowering Fern, Water Fern, and Ditch Fern.

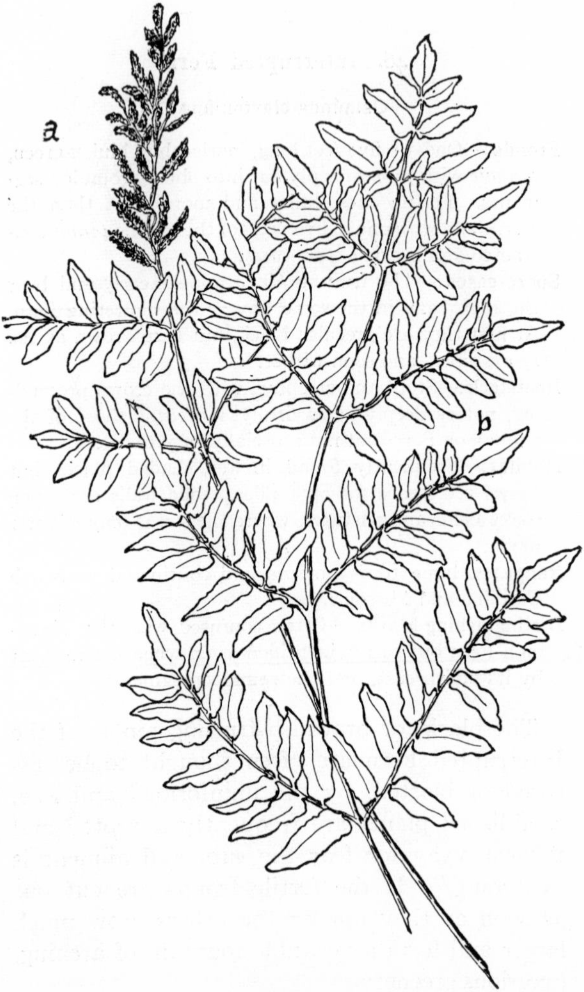

ROYAL FERN

a. Fertile Portion of Fruiting Frond; b. Sterile Frond.

46. Interrupted Fern

Osmúnda claytoniàna

Fronds:—One to five feet long, noticeably bluish-green, *pinnate* with *pinnæ* deeply cut into oblong rounded segments. Fertile ones, taller and more erect than the sterile and with one to five pairs of the middle *pinnæ* contracted and bearing *spore-cases.*

Spore-cases:—The fruiting *pinnæ* appear early and bear the *spore-cases* in the same way as the Flowering Fern. At first they are greenish black, but turn brown as the *spores* ripen, and soon wither.

Rootstock:—Stout and creeping, with the crown protruding, not as deeply or as firmly rooted as those of the Cinnamon Fern, but not especially easy to dig.

Habitat:—Frequently found in wet, shaded places but shows preference for rock piles, stone walls and open rocky fields and pastures, where the soil is only slightly moist.

Range:—Maine to Minnesota and southward to North Carolina and Missouri.

Distinguishing Marks:—Often confused with the Cinnamon Fern but easily identified even when not in fruit by its bluish cast, and the rounded segments.

The black, or brownish fruiting pinnæ of the Interrupted Fern are often thought to be diseased or blasted, by the uninformed and fine, established plants are frequently uprooted and thrown away for fear the supposed ailment is "catching." If the fertile fronds are cut out as soon as they appear the others grow much larger and form a veritable fountain of arching, luxurious greenery.

INTERRUPTED FERN

a. Sterile Portion of Frond; b. Fruiting Pinnæ.

47. Cinnamon Fern

Osmúnda cinnamòmea

Fronds:—The sterile, two to six feet long, *pinnate*, *pinnæ* deeply cut into somewhat scythe-shaped segments terminating in a bluntish, but distinct point. (A pair of opposite segments forms a crescent, suggesting a half-moon, with the horns pointing away from the main stem.) Fertile fronds totally different. They are wand-like, stiff, much shorter, and appear earlier.

Spore-cases:—Entirely cover the contracted, fruiting *pinnæ*. At first bright green, they turn a cinnamon brown in late May and after shedding their *spores*, soon wither, disappearing by the end of June.

Rootstock:—Very large, creeping and covered with a dense, tangled growth of black fibrous roots, which protrudes above the surface and resembles a huge half-buried shoe-brush.

Habitat:—Wherever there are low swampy or boggy areas the Cinnamon Fern is almost certain to abound. It is at its best in shade, but flourishes also in open sun.

Range:—Maine to Florida, west to Minnesota and New Mexico.

Distinguishing Marks:—The exposed "shoe-brush" root, the distinctive fruiting *fronds* and the half-crescent-shaped segments.

The matted rootlets of the Cinnamon Fern, and also those of the Interrupted Fern are widely used for rooting and growing green-house orchids. They are grubbed up, the coarse root-stock extracted and then sawed into slabs of convenient size with a cross-cut saw. The material thus obtained is called Osmundine and thousands of barrels are sold annually. Most of it is collected in New York.

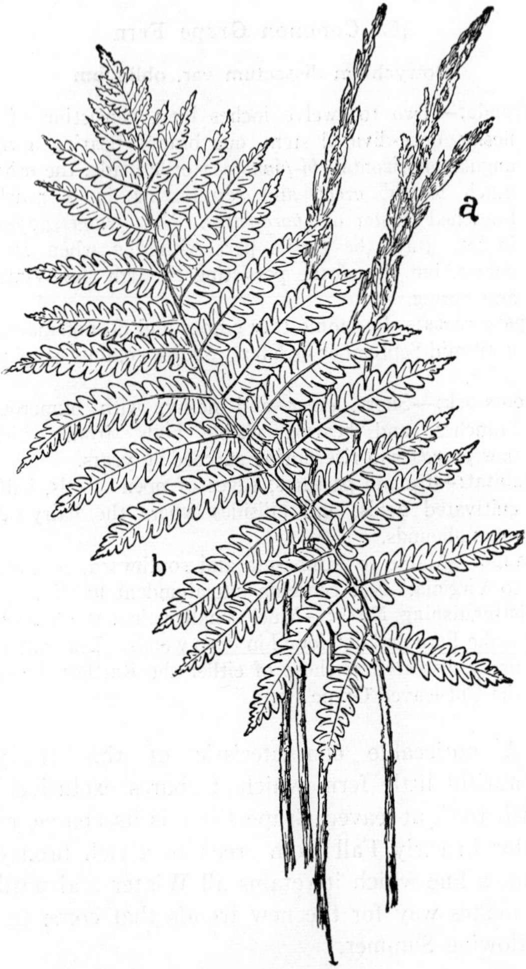

CINNAMON FERN
a. Fertile Frond; b. Sterile Frond.

48. Common Grape Fern

Botrýchium dissectum var. **oblìquum**

Fronds:—Two to twelve inches long, consisting of a fleshy, once-divided stem, one branch bearing a triangular, horizontal, *bi-pinnate*, sterile blade, the other much longer, erect and terminating in a much-branched cluster of *spore-cases.* New *fronds* appear in late July, the fertile part withering when frost comes, but the sterile persisting through the Winter and Spring.

Spore-cases:—Resemble tiny grapes and do not mature until mid-September or later. *Spores* copious, sulphur color.

Rootstock:—Short, erect and fleshy, with numerous branches, and bearing visible buds, from which new *fronds* will rise during succeeding years.

Habitat:—Upland pastures, edges of open woods, half-cultivated fields, and hillsides where the hairy-cap moss abounds.

Range:—Maine to Minnesota and southward, reaching to Virginia. Not common but abundant locally.

Distinguishing Mark:—Much smaller than the Rattlesnake Fern and not found in deep woods. Leaf not so finely dissected as those of either the Rattlesnake or the Cut-leaved Grape Fern.

A noticeable characteristic of this really beautiful little fern, which it shares exclusively with the Cut-leaved Grape Fern, is its change of color in early Fall from green to a rich bronzy tint, a hue which it retains all Winter and until it makes way for the new fronds that come the following Summer.

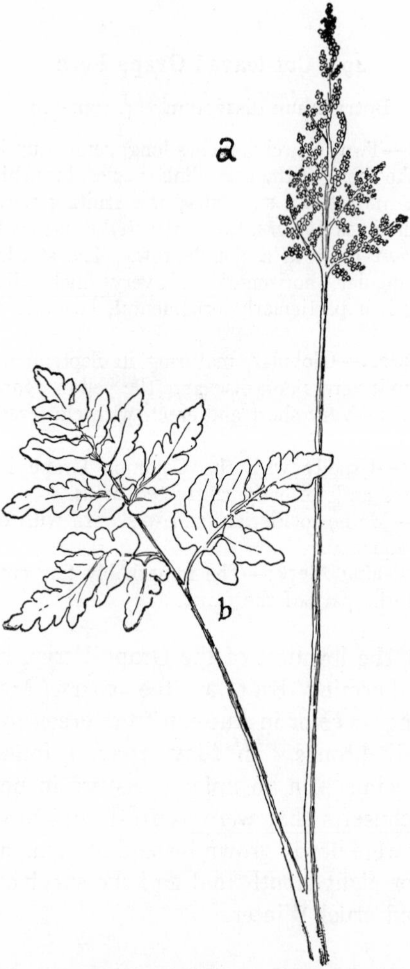

COMMON GRAPE FERN
a. Fertile Section of Frond; b. Sterile Section.

49. Cut-leaved Grape Fern

Botrýchium dissécium var. typicum

Fronds:—Two to twelve inches long, coming up in July, and like those of the preceding species, branching into fertile and sterile segments; the fruiting part twice to four times *pinnate,* the contracted divisions bearing the *spore-cases* in a double row. The sterile blade is triangular, horizontal and very finely dissected, giving it a particularly ornamental, lace-like appearance.

Spore-cases:—Globular, maturing in September, when they split across and discharge the yellow *spores.*

Rootstock:—Very short and erect, with clustered fleshy roots.

Habitat:—Usually with the Common Grape Fern, in pastures and formerly cultivated fields.

Range:—Maine to Florida, and westward with decreasing frequency.

Distinguishing Mark:—The remarkably fine cutting of the sterile part of the *frond.*

This, the loveliest of the Grape Ferns, has the same charming trait as the coarser one, of changing its color in Autumn from green to a sort of ruddy bronze. In May, 1927, I found several specimens in an upland pasture in northern Massachusetts that were as fresh and bronzy as if they were newly grown instead of being at least seven or eight months old and the survivors of a cold and cruel Winter.

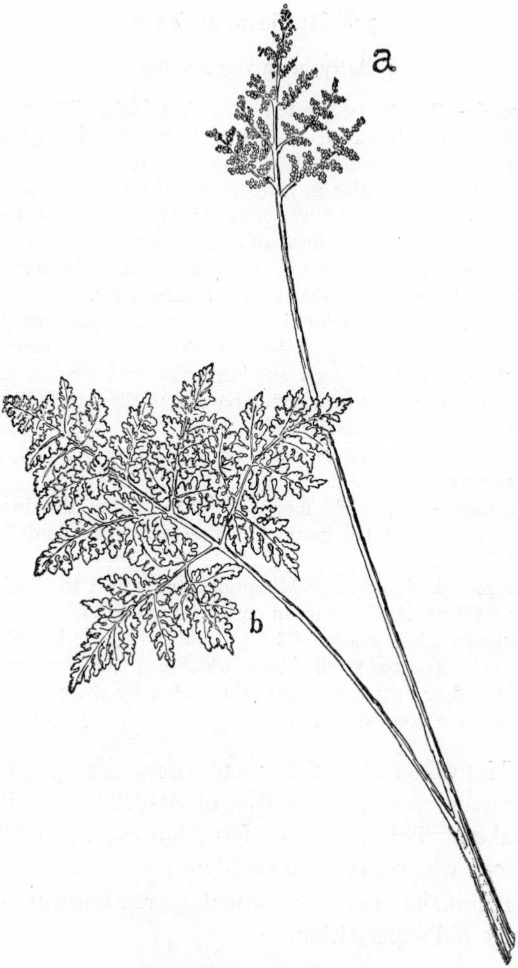

CUT-LEAVED GRAPE FERN

a. Fertile Section of Frond; b. Sterile Section.

50. Rattlesnake Fern

Botrýchium virginiànum

Frond:—One to two, often three feet high. The sterile blade, which spreads horizontally from the fleshy main stem at a considerable distance above the ground, is broadly triangular in shape, and *bi-pinnate* or partly *tri-pinnate,* the *pinnules* again deeply cut into toothed segments. The main stem continues above the sterile blade and branches towards the tip into the narrow twig-like segments that bear the *spore-cases.*

Spore-cases:—Globular in form, splitting transversely, and varying in color from dark yellowish-brown to almost black. *Spores* sulphur color and ripe in late June, after which the fertile portion of the stem withers and practically disappears.

Rootstock:—Short, erect and branching deeply below the surface.

Habitat:—Deep, rich, moist mold in dense, deciduous woods. Soon disappears if in new clearings or planted in full sun.

Range:—Maine west to Minnesota and south to Florida and Texas. Common in congenial localities.

Distinguishing Mark:—The noticeably large, triangular, finely dissected sterile blade, which can hardly be overlooked or mistaken for anything else, by those who go into the deep woods.

Many flowering plants and a few ferns possess common names suggestive of associations with snakes. This beautiful fern, however, inhabits woods where snakes are seldom seen. The name Rattlesnake Fern is probably reminiscent of some old superstition.

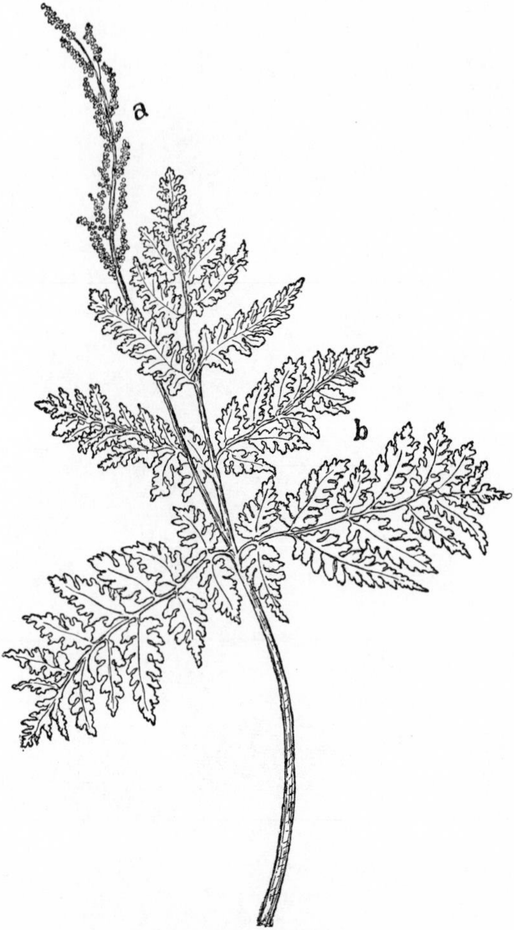

RATTLESNAKE FERN

a. Fertile Section of Frond; b. Sterile Section.

BOTANICAL SYNONYMS

In the following list of scientific names those printed in blackface type are the ones approved by most botanical authorities at the time this revision is printed. The names following these in thin-faced type are synonyms.

BOTANICAL NAMES	COMMON NAMES
1. **Adiantum capillus-veneris**	Venus'-hair Fern
2. **Adiantum pedatum** *Adiantum pedatum* var. *originarium*	Maidenhair Fern
3. **Asplenium platyneuron** *Asplenium ebeneum*	Ebony Spleenwort
4. **Asplenium trichomanes**	Maidenhair Spleenwort
5. **Athyrium angustum** *Athyrium filix-femina* *Asplenium filix-femina*	Northern Lady Fern
6. **Athyrium asplenioides** *Athyrium filix-femina* *Asplenium filix-femina*	Southern Lady Fern
7. **Athyrium pycnocarpon** *Asplenium angustifolium* *Asplenium pycnocarpon* *Diplazium pycnocarpon*	Narrow-leaved Spleenwort
8. **Athyrium thelypteroides** *Diplazium thelypteroides* *Asplenium acrostichoides*	Silvery Spleenwort

9. **Botrichium dissectum var. obliquum** *Botrichium obliquum* *Botrichium ternatum* var. *obliquum*	Common Grape Fern
10. **Botrichium dissectum var. typicum** *Botrichium obliquum* var. *dissectum*	Cut-leaved Grape Fern
11. **Botrichium virginianum** *Osmundopteris virginiana*	Rattlesnake Fern
12. **Camptosorus rhizophyllus**	Walking Fern
13. **Cheilanthes lanosa** *Cheilanthes vestita*	Hairy Lip Fern
14. **Cheilanthes tomentosa**	Wooly Lip Fern
15. **Cryptogramma stelleri** *Pellaea gracilis*	Slender Cliff Brake
16. **Cystopteris bulbifera** *Filix bulbifera*	Bulblet Bladder Fern
17. **Cystopteris fragilis** *Filix fragilis*	Common Bladder Fern
18. **Dennstaedtia punctilobula** *Dicksonia punctilobula* *Dicksonia pilosiuscula*	Hay-scented Fern
19. **Dryopteris boottii** *Aspidium boottii* *Thelypteris boottii*	Boott's Shield Fern
20. **Dryopteris clintoniana** *Dryopteris cristata* var. *clintoniana* *Aspidium cristatum* var. *clintoniana*	Clinton's Shield Fern

21. **Dryopteris cristata** *Aspidium cristatum* *Thelypteris cristata*	Crested Shield Fern
22. **Dryopteris filix-mas** *Aspidium filix-mas* *Thelypteris filix-mas*	Male Fern
23. **Dryopteris goldiana** *Aspidium goldianum* *Thelypteris goldiana*	Goldie's Fern
24. **Dryopteris marginalis** *Aspidium marginale* *Thelypteris marginalis*	Marginal Shield Fern
25. **Dryopteris noveboracensis** *Aspidium noveboracense* *Thelypteris noveboracensis*	New York Fern
26. **Dryopteris simulata** *Aspidium simulata* *Thelypteris simulata*	Massachusetts Fern
27. **Dryopteris spinulosa** *Aspidium spinulosum* *Thelypteris spinulosa*	Spinulose Shield Fern
28. **Dryopteris spinulosa** var. **americana** *Dryopteris campyloptera* *Thelypteris spinulosa* var. *americana*	Mountain Shield Fern
29. **Dryopteris spinulosa** var. **intermedia** *Dryopteris intermedia* *Aspidium spinulosum* var. *intermedium*	American Shield Fern

30. **Dryopteris thelypteris** *Aspidium thelypteris* *Thelypteris palustris*	Marsh Fern
31. **Onoclea sensibilis**	Sensitive Fern
32. **Osmunda cinnamomea**	Cinnamon Fern
33. **Osmunda claytoniana**	Interrupted Fern
34. **Osmunda regalis** *Osmunda regalis* var. *spectabilis*	Royal Fern
35. **Pellaea atropurpurea**	Purple Cliff Brake
36. **Phegopteris dryopteris** *Dryopteris dryopteris* *Dryopteris linnaeana* *Thelypteris dryopteris*	Oak Fern
37. **Phegopteris hexagonoptera** *Dryopteris hexagonoptera* *Thelypteris hexagonoptera*	Broad Beech Fern
38. **Phegopteris polypodioides** *Dryopteris phegopteris* *Thelypteris phegopteris*	Long Beech Fern
39. **Polypodium polypodioides** *Polypodium incanum*	Resurrection Fern
40. **Polypodium virginianum** *Polypodium vulgare*	Common Polypody
41. **Polystichum acrostichoides** *Dryopteris acrostichoides* *Aspidium acrostichoides*	Christmas Fern
42. **Polystichum braunii**	Braun's Holly Fern

43. **Pclystichum lonchitis** *Aspidium lonchitis*	Mountain Holly Fern
44. **Pteretis nodulosa** *Onoclea struthiopteris* *Matteuccia struthiopteris*	Ostrich Fern
45. **Pteridium aquilinum** var. **lutiusculum** *Pteridium latiusculum* *Pteris aquilina*	Bracken
46. **Woodsia glabella**	Smooth Woodsia
47. **Woodsia ilvensis**	Rusty Woodsia
48. **Woodsia obtusa**	Blunt-lobed Woodsia
49. **Woodwardia areolata** *Lorinseria areolata* *Woodwardia angustifolia*	Narrow-leaved Chain Fern
50. **Woodwardia virginica** *Anchistea virginica*	Virginia Chain Fern

WHEN THE SPORES ARE RIPE

The dates given are approximate and were compiled by Mr. Raynal Dodge for his book *The Ferns and Fern Allies of New England.* They are likely to fall a few days earlier south of the latitude of New York.

American Maidenhair	August 10
Berry Bladderfern	July 25
Bracken	September 5
Boott Woodfern	July 10
Braun Hollyfern	August 10
Brittle Fern	July 5
Christmas Fern	July 5
Cinnamon Fern	May 30
Clinton Woodfern	July 30
Common Polypody	August 10
Common Woodfern	June 30
Common Woodsia	July 20
Crested Woodfern	July 10
Cutleaf Grapefern	September 15
Ebony Spleenwort	August 20
Goldie Fern	July 30
Grapefern	September 15
Hairy Lipfern	August 5
Hay-scented Fern	August 20
Interrupted Fern	May 25
Leather Woodfern	July 30
Lowland Lady Fern	August 5

Maidenhair Spleenwort	August 20
Male Fern	July 25
Marshfern	August 30
Massachusetts Fern	September 15
Mountain Hollyfern	August 5
Mountain Woodfern	June 30
Narrow Beechfern	July 10
Narrowleaf Chainfern	September 30
Narrowleaf Spleenwort	September 10
New York Fern	August 20
Oakfern	June 30
Ostrich Fern	June 5
Purple Cliffbrake	July 25
Rattlesnake Fern	June 25
Resurrection Fern	July 25
Royal Fern	June 20
Rusty Woodsia	August 15
Sensitive Fern	September 15
Silvery Spleenwort	August 15
Slender Rockbrake	July 20
Smooth Woodsia	August 10
Southern Maidenhair	July 30
Toothed Woodfern	June 30
Upland Lady Fern	August 5
Virginia Chainfern	July 10
Walking Fern	August 5
Winged Beechfern	August 25
Woolly Lipfern	August 5

HOW TO MAKE A FERN HERBARIUM

(Adapted from an article by Miss F. E. Corne in *The American Fern Journal.*)

The making of an herbarium is a very agreeable pastime, but requires careful handling and tasteful arrangement when mounting the specimens.

On collecting tours, even if not going far, take a sharp knife and something in which to carry your finds. For short distances a newspaper may be sufficient. Never hold in the warm hand a frond which you are intending to press and mount, as the delicate lower pinnæ or leaflets are apt to get injured, and specimens when mounted should be as perfect as possible. Besides, some of the sturdiest fronds, like those of the Sensitive Fern, wilt very quickly after they are gathered, and the warmth of the hand hastens the process. Be careful to get the entire stem, and if possible, especially if small, a bit of the rootstock also, as this adds to the value of the specimen and helps to identify the species. With very small plants, if they are plentiful and not so rare that you are committing vandalism, get a whole one, root and all. Wash off while still soft any earth which may adhere to the roots, as later when pressed and dry it will form an unsightly mass which cannot be removed. Be sure to gather both sterile and

fertile fronds if possible and tie them together with a bit of string, or place those of each fern in separate papers to prevent confusion later. It is also well to have on hand some slips of paper on which to record at once the date, place of gathering and other data of interest.

For long trips a good sized portfolio, not less than 13 X 17 inches, containing sheets of damp paper, is indispensable for carrying and preserving the ferns. The one important thing of course, is to keep the gathered fronds from withering until they are put in press.

On reaching home, if any fronds are actually shrivelled and dry, they are of course useless, but if only wilted, throw them into a tub of water and leave them there for a few hours, or over night if you like, and next day you will find that they have regained their original freshness and beauty. Before pressing them, however, the extra moisture should be carefully removed with a soft cloth, or blotter; and the absorbent paper in the press should be changed within a few hours. A press made for the purpose, which can be bought for a moderate sum, is the best kind; and with it should be ordered several quires of white absorbent paper and a quantity of gray blotting paper.

When ready to put them in press, arrange the gathered specimens as gracefully as possible, each with its label beside it, within folded sheets of white absorbent paper. Carefully straighten out with a fine brush or small pointed stick any crumpled pinnules. Each folded sheet containing fronds should be placed between two of

the gray blotting paper, then a sheet of corrugated pasteboard, then the gray paper again and so on. The gray blotters should be changed for fresh dry ones at least once during the first twenty-four hours, and it is well to change them again two or three times during the next few days. Damp blotters should be dried in the sun or other warm place before re-using. The filled press should also be left in a warm place to hasten the drying process and help preserve the color. Specimens should be left untouched in the white paper sheets until quite dry, changing only the gray blotters. When the last suspicion of moisture has evaporated the specimens are ready for mounting.

The pages for the herbarium should be uniform as regards size and kind of paper. Regulation mounting sheets are 11½ × 16½ inches. The rule is to have only one specimen to each page. Fasten the fronds and stems with short narrow strips of gummed paper, or courtplaster.

Assemble the mounted sheets, in convenient groups, in covers made of thick manila paper, and write a "table of contents" on the front page of each cover. Keep them in a substantially made portfolio, or in one of the boxes made for the purpose that can be obtained from makers of botanical equipment.

HOW TO GROW THE FERNS

Directions for their Culture and Care in the Open Ground, on the Porch and in the House.

GROWING FERNS IN THE OPEN

"Give Ferns what they need, and as they need it," says an article in the *American Fern Journal*, "and they will amply repay all your care. Shade, moisture, good soil and some stones are necessary for all, but each species also has individual likings for other things, just as people have. If a fern grows naturally in a wet, rocky place it cannot be expected to thrive in a dry, stoneless garden bed. Nor will one whose natural habit is to carry its crown well above the ground, be likely to flourish if the crown is buried. Any one who is lucky enough to own a bit of moist woodland may accomplish wonders with ferns. And those less fortunate can always coax some of the stronger growers to make a brave showing, even in a city backyard!"

The best time to transplant Ferns from the woods and fields is in late spring or early summer when they have about reached maturity and can be replanted with due regard to relative height and artistic effect. A safe method of digging them and carrying them home is to lift the roots carefully, wash off the soil in a nearby brook or pool and wrap them, first, in a layer of dampened moss taken from a fallen log or the sloping sides of a boulder, then with two thicknesses of ordinary newspaper. A surprising number of plants thus handled can be packed in an ordinary

market basket, where they will remain in good condition for planting for several days—even a week or two, if kept in a cool, shaded spot. Should any of the fronds be broken during the move new ones will usually grow and replace them in a short time.

For planting purposes Ferns may be divided into two classes—those with slender branching rootstocks which creep more or less extensively, usually at or just below the surface: and those with short, thick rootstocks which terminate in a more or less prominent crown. The former spread rapidly and make large, dense colonies, sending up numerous fronds in Spring and continuing to produce them at intervals of a few inches apart during the growing season. The Common Polypody and the New York Fern are notable examples of this class. The kinds with thick rootstocks bear their fronds in more or less circular tufts, rising from the crowns only. Here belong the Shield Ferns, the Christmas Fern, the Ostrich Fern and others. Many of the rock ferns like the Maidenhair Spleenwort and the Walking Fern are also in this class, but their rootstocks are small and roundish with bunches of matted, spreading rootlets issuing from the bottom, and their planting is a simple proceeding.

It is important to see that rootstocks are placed in the ground in their natural positions. Don't bury the crowns if you find them protruding like those of the Marginal Shield Fern; and don't cover surface creepers with several inches of soil. It is just as easy to plant them right and failure to do so is inviting disaster.

As regards soil, nearly all Ferns prefer one rich in leaf mold, with a liberal proportion of sand and kept constantly moist. The best way to insure the right amount of moisture at all times is to maintain a mulch of half-decayed leaves, applying it at the time of planting. A mulch keeps the garden hose idle except during protracted dry spells. It should vary in thickness according to the size and natural habits of the plants—an inch or two during the summer months and twice or three times as thick during winter. Mosses and creeping or tufted plants, like the Partridgeberry, the tiny white Violet and the Bluet or Quaker Lady, make effective and lovely mulches.

Nearly all Ferns demand some degree of shade. Note their preferences at the time of digging and do your best to suit them in this regard. Special cultural hints are given in connection with the descriptions and habitat photographs of the Ferns featured in this book, where the foregoing general directions are not entirely adequate.

GROWING FERNS INDOORS IN SUMMER

There are a number of native Ferns that do well indoors and on verandas during the summer months, if planted in suitable receptacles and given attention when needed. I say *suitable* receptacles because of the tendency of many to buy or contrive gaudily painted or bizarre contraptions that distract attention from the beauty and decorative effect of the growing things they contain. Good taste requires that fern pots and boxes and other containers be as inconspicuous in color and shape as it is possible to make them.

Those who are blessed with an artistic sense have a fine opportunity to exercise it, when it comes to choosing the most fitting ferns for different uses. If for a centerpiece, on a stand or table, for example, the basket form of young Cinnamon or Interrupted Ferns is ideal, but they must be young plants. And the long, slender drooping fronds of the Bulblet Bladder Fern, that hang or ramble down steep, rocky banks and cliffs, are unsurpassed for draping pots and brackets, and festooning along the fronts of window or porch boxes. I have been an occasional visitor to two summer hotels, where much of their attractiveness is due to boxes covered with rough brown cedar or hemlock bark, filled with different woodferns and their

sides half concealed by pendant fronds of Bulblet Bladder Ferns and Long Beech Ferns. These boxes are everywhere,—in the lobby, the dining-room, the parlors and on the porches.

Ferns for summer decoration should not be dug before the first of June, or until they have developed a sufficiently strong growth to stand the shock of transplanting. At this time, too, they are at their best and brightest, and near enough to maturity to make it possible to judge of their ultimate size.

Drainage and continuous moisture are the chief essentials to successful culture. Whether boxes, pots, or baskets are used as containers, there should be two inches of pebbles, or better, broken charcoal at the bottom. Cover this with a dense layer of woods, or sphagnum moss, then fill with black woods dirt, mixing in a liberal quantity of clean sand. After planting, cover the surface with live moss. Water thoroughly but not too frequently. Set those that are movable out in the open during gentle rains and shelter all of them from strong winds, which are apt to play havoc with the delicate fronds.

Excellent kinds for summer planting are any of the Shield Ferns, the Christmas Fern, the Bulblet Bladder Fern, the Narrow-leaved Spleenwort, the Maidenhair, the Long Beech Fern and the Oak Fern. The Mountain Shield Fern is particularly fine with its broad, plumy, dark green fronds and the American Shield Fern is almost equally desirable. Both are easily dug and ask only ordinary care. The Christmas Fern is charming in combination with the Maidenhair

and if its fertile fronds are cut out when the fruit-dots appear, the sterile fronds will become more luxuriant and keep longer.

Ferns grown indoors during summer will, if planted in shady, protected nooks in the Fall, benefit by the Winter rest, regain lost vigor and be in fine condition for re-use the following year.

A TERRARIUM

WILD FERNS IN THE HOUSE

Several of the native ferns do well in the house during the winter. The Common Polypody, the Maidenhair Spleenwort, the Ebony Spleenwort, and the Purple Cliff Brake stand the dry atmosphere and heat of most living rooms better than any others. If they are to survive for any considerable time, however, they should stand in a cool corner, protected from the sun, and be sprayed with clear water as often as once or twice a day.

A Terrarium, or Wardian case, is an admirable device for growing small and delicate species of native ferns indoors. It is a sort of baby conservatory—a miniature glass house—that when planted and placed on a table or stand, is a tasteful ornament of fascinating interest for any room. A rectangular aquarium, like that shown in the illustration, makes an entirely satisfactory Terrarium if fitted with a removable glass top that any picture framer can make and fit. The fern case should be equipped and planted for the winter during the month of October. Put an inch or two of broken stone in the bottom and cover it with a layer of moss; Sphagnum is the best kind to use. Have ready a bucketful of leaf mold mixed with sand and pile it on the moss to the depth of an inch around the edges, shaping it in the center into an irregu-

lar mound four or five inches high at its crest. On this mound arrange a number of weather-worn rocks that will look all the better if they are adorned with patches of lichen. Leave as many soil pockets among the stones as possible, in which to plant the ferns.

The four kinds of ferns I have mentioned are perfectly at home in a Terrarium, and there are several others that will do equally well, but which would perish very quickly in an ordinary house atmosphere. Particularly good kinds are the Walking Fern, the Slender Cliff Brake, the Oak Fern, the Rusty Woodsia, and tiny first year plants of the Cinnamon Fern, the Interrupted Fern, and the Marginal Shield. The arrangement of the kinds that are chosen is a matter of personal taste and the only suggestion I have to make is that the planting should not be overdone. Just enough ferns to about half-conceal the stones would be right. One good watering at the time of planting should suffice for the winter, if supplemented by light weekly sprayings to keep the foliage fresh without adding to the volume of moisture in the bottom of the case. At the time of the weekly spraying the lid of the case may be left open an inch or two for a while, for ventilation.

Aside from the original arrangement and planting a Terrarium practically takes care of itself, and will afford a remarkable amount of pleasure with a minimum amount of trouble if one enjoys watching the daily growth of plants.

EXOTIC HOUSE FERNS IN WINTER

In order to grow exotic or greenhouse ferns successfully in the house during winter, perfect drainage must be provided and reasonable care taken to supply water as needed, but without over-watering. These are the two prime requisites. As for soil, there is nothing better than a mixture of fibrous loam, leaf mold and sand, equal parts of each. Suitable potting soil for ferns can be obtained at any greenhouse if the ingredients named are not available.

Cleanliness is also necessary to health and a luxuriant growth. Daily showering with a fine spray is excellent practice. The plants should be protected from direct sunshine and from exposure to drafts. The best way to water house ferns is to plunge the pot to the brim in a tub of water and leave it there for fifteen or twenty minutes, not longer. This will thoroughly saturate the ball of earth around the roots.

Keep the atmosphere of the room moist. It is as necessary for the health of the family as it is for the plants. Pans kept filled with water and placed on the radiators will do the work. You can get them at any hardware store. Some are made to hang behind the radiator, out of

sight. Shallow bowls on a sunny windowsill will help, and can be kept filled with narcissus and other flowering bulbs.

If the house air is too dry, the ferns are likely to become infested with insect pests. If so, immediate action is necessary to prevent them from multiplying and destroying the beauty or even the life of affected plants. Spraying the fronds on both sides with clear cold water will rout red spider. The green aphis, or plant louse, can be abolished by a spray of "Black-leaf 40," which is also effective in getting rid of the pesky little white flies, if applied in time. Scale on the underside of fronds and on the stems can be killed by touching each one with a tooth-pick or fine-pointed camel's hair brush dipped in lemon or fir tree oil. Follow this treatment a day later by first sponging the plants with Ivory soapsuds and then giving them a thorough rinsing with clear water.

There are three kinds of "florist" ferns that can be depended upon to do well in the winter home if given a reasonable amount of care. First and foremost is the omnipresent Boston fern—a native of the tropics that abounds in the wilds of southern Florida, where it usually grows on the trunks of Palm trees. This robust plant endures with equanimity either the dry heat of living rooms or the chill of store windows. All it asks for, in order to thrive, and develop enormous fronds, is a light porous soil, plenty of water at the roots and a weekly shower bath above. It will, however, go waterless for days without apparent injury. There are about

fifty varieties of this fern, most of them with elaborately cut, plumy fronds, but few with anything like the stamina of their lusty parent.

The second of the "florist" ferns that takes kindly to house culture is the Holly fern, known technically as *Cyrtomium falcatum*. It has glossy, dark green, spiny fronds and is not difficult to please culturally. Give it a soil composed largely of leaf mold, a moderate supply of water and an occasional rest of a few weeks in a cool dark room, or cellar, and it will flourish indefinitely. It will tolerate a lower temperature than the Boston fern.

The third fern that makes good as a house plant *if* its cultural needs are supplied is one of the Maidenhairs whose trade name is *Adiantum cuneatum*. Its growth is strikingly decorative and plumy and it is ideal as a centerpiece. It requires more attention, however, than either of the others, particularly as regards watering, for if the soil is allowed to become dry, the fronds quickly wither. It repays intelligent care, however, by living for years.

If one possesses a conservatory, large or small, or even an enclosed room of some sort in which an equable temperature and a constantly moist atmosphere can be maintained, there are many other tender ferns well worth trying, especially *Adiantum farleyense*, a Maidenhair from the Barbadoes that is extremely beautiful and closely resembles our native Southern Maidenhair.

HOW TO RAISE FERNS FROM SPORES

Growing ferns from spores is one of the most interesting experiences imaginable and not at all difficult. The spores can be collected from any woodland species in midsummer and they will germinate if scattered on any kind of porous surface, like moist peat or sand, provided it is kept moist and warm. The best way to proceed is to take a fern dish or bulb pan and fill it half full of broken flower-pots or pebbles. On top of this lay a thin sheet of moss, then add about an inch of finely sifted, sandy leaf mold. This should be sterilized by placing the dish or pan in an oven and baking for half an hour. Then, when cool enough, and made thoroughly moist but not wet, mix the spores with a little fine sand and sprinkle them evenly over the surface. Press down gently with a block of smooth wood, cover the pan with a pane of glass, set it in a basin of water and leave it in a warm, dark place for several days. It may then be brought into the light, but never into sunshine. The soil must not be allowed to become dry, and must never be watered from above. Drops of moisture that accumulate on the under side of the pane of glass should be removed every day. In from a few days to a week or so, according to the species, a scum-like coat resembling green

mildew will appear on the surface and if examined under a strong pocket lens this coat will be seen to be composed of prothallia. And if the prothallia are watched closely the tiny fronds of the young fern will soon be visible to the naked eye.

As soon as these first small fronds are large enough to be handled they should be transplanted in clumps of four or five each to boxes filled with finely sifted soil, composed of one-half rich garden loam and one-half leaf mold. Sufficient space should be allowed between the clumps to give them a better chance to form rootlets and to make it easier to separate them later on. When the plants have made two or three fronds each they should be again transplanted into similar boxes and allowed to remain until they are large enough to be transferred into two or two and a quarter inch pots. The most convenient boxes for holding transplanted ferns are four inches deep, fourteen inches wide and twenty-two inches long. A box of these dimensions will hold about two hundred plants spaced an inch apart.

WILD FERNS FOR SPECIAL USES

For Moist Shaded Nooks and Corners

American Maidenhair
Northern Lady Fern
Christmas Fern
Male Fern
American Shield Fern
Narrow-leaved Spleenwort
Royal Fern
Clinton's Shield Fern
Goldie's Fern
Mountain Shield Fern

For Moist Sunny Locations

Cinnamon Fern
Ostrich Fern
Narrow-leaved Chain Fern
Interrupted Fern
Southern Lady Fern
Cut-leaved Grape Fern

For the Rock Garden, in Shade

Ebony Spleenwort
Venus-hair Fern
Common Polypody
Hairy Lip Fern
Braun's Holly Fern
Marginal Shield Fern
Oak Fern
Bulblet Bladder Fern
Maidenhair Spleenwort
Walking Fern
Resurrection Fern
Woolly Lip Fern
Mountain Holly Fern
Clinton's Shield Fern
Blunt-lobed Woodsia
Common Bladder Fern

For the Rock Garden, in Sun

Rusty Woodsia
Purple Cliff Brake

For Massing and Underplanting

New York Fern
Long Beech Fern
Broad Beech Fern
Bulblet Bladder Fern

For Window and Porch Boxes and Summer Decorations Indoors

Bulblet Bladder Fern
Braun's Holly Fern
American Shield Fern
Christmas Fern
Mountain Holly Fern
Mountain Shield Fern

For Winter Culture Indoors

Common Polypody
Maidenhair Spleenwort
Purple Cliff Brake
Ebony Spleenwort

For Terraria

Walking Fern
Purple Cliff Brake
Ebony Spleenwort
Rusty Woodsia
Maidenhair Spleenwort
Slender Cliff Brake
Oak Fern
Blunt-lobed Woodsia

Undesirables in Any Garden

Bracken
Sensitive Fern
Hay-scented Fern
Marsh Fern

BOOKS USEFUL IN THE STUDY OF FERNS

Broun, Maurice, *Index to North American Ferns,* Published by compiler, Orleans, Mass., 1938.

Chrysler, Mintin A., and Edwards, J. L., *The Ferns of New Jersey,* Rutgers Univ. Press, New Brunswick, N. J., 1947.

Clute, Willard N., *Our Ferns, Their Haunts, Habits, and Folklore,* Frederick A. Stokes Co., New York, 1938.

Durand, Herbert, *Field Book of Common Ferns,* G. P. Putnam's Sons, New York, Revised Edition 1949.

———, *Wild Flowers and Ferns,* G. P. Putnam's Sons, New York, 1925.

Eastman, Helen, *New England Ferns and Their Common Allies,* Houghton Mifflin Co., New York, 1904.

Parsons, Frances T., *How to Know the Ferns,* Chas. Scribner's Sons, New York, 1902.

Slosson, Margaret, *How Ferns Grow,* Henry Holt and Co., New York, 1906.

Tilton, George H., *The Fern Lover's Companion,* Little, Brown and Co., Boston, 1927.

Waters, Campbell E., *Ferns—A Manual for the Northeastern States,* Henry Holt and Co., New York, 1908.

Wherry, Edgar T., *Guide to Eastern Ferns,* The Science Press Printing Co., Lancaster, Pa., 1948.

Wiley, Farida A., *Ferns of Northeastern United States*, American Museum of Natural History, New York, 1936.

Woolson, Grace A., *How to Grow the Ferns*, Doubleday, Page and Co., Garden City, Long Island, N. Y., 1902.

General Botanies Which Also Treat of Ferns

Gray's New Manual of Botany, Seventh Edition, Revised by Benjamin L. Robinson and Merritt L. Fernald, American Book Co., New York, 1908.

Britton and Brown, *Illustrated Flora of the United States and Canada*, Chas. Scribner's Sons, New York, Revised Edition 1949.

Periodicals Dealing with Ferns

American Fern Journal, Published quarterly by the American Fern Society, N. Queen St. & McGovern Ave., Lancaster, Pa.

Bulletin of the Torrey Botanical Club, Published bimonthly by the Torrey Botanical Club. The Science Press Printing Co., N. Queen St. & McGovern Ave., Lancaster, Pa.

INDEX

INDEX

INDEX